DEDICATION

All praise and glory to God.

With love to Grandpa,

Dr. A.P.J. Abdul Kalam.

With thanks to my wife Mahjabeen

and children Afraz, Afeef and Nazneen.

AUTHOR'S NOTE

Dr. A.P.J. Abdul Kalam has been an integral part of my life. That too everyone who knew about this connection advised me to follow his footsteps. Many of my friends followed Dr. Abdul Kalam, some kept his photo along with the deities. I also followed him by coincidence on many of the important elements in his life path. I studied at Schwartz Matriculation Higher Secondary School at Ramanathapuram. Grandpa did his studies at the Tamil medium version of it. When I landed up for my Masters in Engineering at Madras Institute of Technology (MIT), Chennai, many believed that he was the one who influenced me to go there. I did the unthinkable of selecting Manufacturing Engineering over Aeronautical Engineering. But he was gracious enough to say "I was in the old hostel and where are you staying?". I stayed in Birla Hostel.

When I completed my masters, I didn't make it to the software industry. I failed in the campus interview of the Indian Space Research Organisation (ISRO). I did not apply for a job at the Defense Research Development Organisation (DRDO). I was trying to get a job in the manufacturing industry in Coimbatore

CONTENT

Title of Book:
Greatness Unlimited
Learning from the life of Dr. A.P.J. Abdul Kalam.

Name of Author/Editor:
Gulaam Khwaja Moinudeen AKPM

This edition published on October 2019

ISBN : 978-93-5391-473-8

Copyright:

Name & Address of Publisher:
Gulaam Khwaja Moinudeen AKPM
Park View Apartments, Haines Road, Frazer Town
Bengaluru -560005

Name & Address of Printer: **Pothi.com**
Mudranik Technologies Pvt Ltd # 634, Ground Floor,
5th Main, Indiranagar 2nd Stage, Bangalore 560038

area. By that time Dr. Abdul Kalam was the 11th President of India. His colleague Dr. Y S Rajan referred me to the Confederation of Indian Industry (CII) led by Mr. Tarun Das. CII was willing to give me a job. This was at that period of time when many assumed being part of President's family one need not have a job or it is a nuisance to employ such people. I am extremely thankful to CII where I spent nearly 15 years of professional life at various capacities. The confidence for writing this book comes from my work at CII and from the support of Dr. A.P.J. Abdul Kalam.

By the time I finished my interview my oncoming manager got promoted and moved to Delhi. I was then offered a job at CII, Delhi. This is when by coincidence I spent the best years of my life with Dr. Abdul Kalam while he was the President of India. We discussed many ideas, argued about petty things, and made fun of ourselves.

It is a difficult journey being part of an overachiever's family. He influenced my thinking and decision making. It was very hard to live alongside the Sufi saint in him. He had very fewer things in his possession. I was a young man just started working. This was the dichotomy of life. The scientific side of him was very sharp. I had to read a lot to keep pace with him. I read many of his favorite books so that I am able to participate in the wonderful conversations.

To further go deep into this unique relationship I have to mention that I was one of his 22 grandsons from the combined family. But he had a special place for me in his heart. He always found time to visit my house in Chennai and Bengaluru. His love showed when he invited my family several times to stay with him at his residence post-retirement at 10, Rajaji Marg, New Delhi.

It was this thread of life that brought me on the fateful day of 28th July 2015 to New Delhi. I waited at 10, Rajaji Marg with immeasurable emptiness in my heart for his mortal remains to arrive. I along with my family travelled till Rameswaram where we laid him to rest.

It has been more than 4 years but I am yet to come to terms with the fact that he is no more. I still feel his aura around me. I still hear the child-like giggle and see his Saint like smile. He may not lead or favor me, but his love would take me through the rest of my life.

There are numerous books about Dr. Abdul Kalam and each might end up telling the same story from a different angle. I am presenting one such angle and bring some untold stories. Many of the quotes mentioned in the books are told personally to me. They may not be famous but meant a world to me. This book is an attempt to present the greatness he displayed in every aspect of life.

- Gulaam Khwaja Moinudeen

PROLOGUE

A grandfather was standing before his friend Arjuna, a tree more than 100 years old. He was not the world-renowned scientist nor a former President of India at that moment. He was not even the person who carries love received from every section of India. He was just a grandfather. He wanted to know from his friend what would it take to bring back his grandson who is fighting for his life. The life support system is running in full blast as his grandson's lungs have failed to respond. He thought about his great-grand-children, tiny little boys and his eyes became moist. He asked his friend Arjuna what should he do? Is there a way where he could change the future. Arjuna stood still for some time and then whispered something. The grandfather walked back to his office with a smile on his face.

I opened my eyes. I was not able to see anything clearly. I could hear a lot of sounds. It came back to me suddenly that I was in a Hospital. I tried to get up. I could not even move. I saw the nurse telling me "please don't move, you have been through a lot". I could not see a clock or calendar. I realized I was in a Critical Care Unit. I tried speaking but the words were not coming out. I could see a lot of tubes connected to me. My throat had a connection to the ventilator and that was why I could not speak.

The doctors rushed to my side. They tried to speak to me. I felt like floating. They asked me to take rest. When my wife visited, I asked her through signs "Have I been sleeping for three days?". The nurse in the CCU almost dropped something from her hand hearing that question. Everyone kept saying "You take rest". I asked for a pen and paper and wrote a message for my doctor. This act astonished the doctor. It was not a surprise that after so many years of education, I always knew how to write.

I kept hearing Dr. A.P.J. Abdul Kalam was coming to see me. My entire family was visiting me at different times. It was very funny to see my wife wearing a protective gown, gloves etc and entering my room like in Hollywood science fiction movies. I started remembering getting into Apollo Hospitals Chennai in early Oct 2013. I returned from Australia from a business trip carrying an unknown virus.

When I woke up again after a brief nap, I saw Dr. A.P.J. Abdul

Kalam, my grandfather sitting near my bed and smiling at me. He then told me that I was asleep for more than 15 days with life support.

It was early 2015 and I was standing with Dr. A.P.J. Abdul Kalam before Arjuna. He was thinking deeply. Arjuna was standing still and swaying to the breeze as if to answer only to him. He asked me to make a wish. I told him that I want him to see my seven-year-old son going to college. He didn't answer for a long time. He finally said, "You are asking for too much". •

MISSILE MAN

> "Don't filter people, I want to meet all"
>
> *- Dr. A.P.J. Abdul Kalam*

Rameswaram, the island town was so colorful that day preparing to welcome the son of the soil, the Missile man, Dr. A.P.J. Abdul Kalam. I hardly knew how big he was in the late 1980s. My mother told me how important he is for the family as well as for the Nation. Already my maternal grandfather's house was filling up with relatives and friends. Police cordoned off the area. The bomb squad brought in a big dog and scanners. I was in-charge of taking them around the house. I followed the dog with big eyes that went through every room with a look of authority.

When that finished, the obvious question from Police was whether Dr. Abdul Kalam would eat at the house. When the answer was affirmative, they told me they wanted samples of every food item. I was to coordinate when the food was ready and help Police to get the samples. Meanwhile, there was a call on the landline which I attended. The caller identified himself as an officer from CBI (Could have been any-body though!). But I was so proud, I almost came to attention. They told me that I have to attend calls and keep updating until Dr. Abdul Kalam reached the house. I checked with elders and they all said it is genuine.

Dr. Abdul Kalam arrived in an Ambassador car with police cars before and after. He was wearing a simple dress but a brilliant smile. He waved to people standing around him. I was completely unaware of why he was that famous. But I thought to myself maybe he did something that all the people waving at him are proud of. He soon came inside the house. Even without giving time for him to go to freshen up everyone wanted to meet him at the same time.

My mother took me to him and introduced. He always called me "Gulaam Sahib" (I have hardly seen him address even a new-born child without respect). He asked me a lot of questions about my academics, interests, sports and my aim in life. He was very happy when my mother told him I am good in

"My mother told me how important he is for the family as well as for the Nation. Already my maternal grandfather's house was filling up with relatives and friends."

academics and good in mathematics. I was a small-town kid and didn't know what to even ask him. I never realized my first life lesson would come from him before the day ended.

I got busy with providing samples next. The police collected food meant for Grandpa in small transparent plastic bags. I innocently asked whether someone would eat and test. I never got an answer for that except big smiles from police officers.

Meanwhile, the fans of Dr. Abdul Kalam thronged him. I had to attend to some requests from the Police and went outside the house. Whenever Dr. Abdul Kalam visited, this is how I became the coordinator for Police/ Security. I saw some small children without shirts and holding a small piece of paper waiting outside. They called me and told me that they wanted to meet Dr. Abdul Kalam and were not allowed inside. I went inside and asked my Grandpa Dr. Abdul Kalam. He looked at me deeply and said "Don't filter people by their looks and status. Quickly call them inside. We don't know which future leader is hiding among them".

I escorted those children inside and they got autographs in the small piece of papers. He asked them with great interest about their present life, why they came to meet him and their aim in life. I was struck by the way he spoke to them with great happiness and undivided attention. It was my first ever lesson and live demonstration of humbleness from Dr. Abdul Kalam.

We had then a few photographs taken where he was wearing his white dhoti. I stood behind him and with other cousins. This photo is part of the book "Wings of Fire", which again shows how simple he was and how well he connected with family. That photo reminds me of the lessons I learned from him during that visit.

One fine day my father told that we have to go and make a phone call to Grandpa. We went to the telecom office and my father filled out a form. We waited for half an hour. I later learned it was Trunk Call Booking. I got my chance and I heard a long hello (helloooooooo!) followed by Gulaam Sahib. This long hello remained with me for the next three decades.

I later learned the call was to discuss the trip of my maternal grandfather to visit Dr. Abdul Kalam at Hyderabad. We traveled to Chennai from Rameswaram and then to Hyderabad in Charminar Express. By this time I got used to long train travels due to my father serving in the Army.

We traveled by car and after some time we entered a heavily fortified area. After some rigorous checking, we were inside DRDL Hyderabad (Defense Research & Development Laboratory). We settled in the Guest house and started waiting for Dr. Abdul Kalam to visit us. This visit involved my earliest days of getting close to him and he getting to know me.

I got dazzled when Grandpa took me inside the lab. Scientists were busily working on a big cylinder connected with tons of wires. He asked me what I was seeing. Then he went on explaining that the scientists are working on the fuel tank of Agni missile. I learned about various elements of the missile. The elements worked in tandem to deliver the missile to the precise location. He was a little upset that I didn't ask many questions.

He told me, "You have to continuously acquire knowledge. Whenever you encounter something new, ask questions". It was a lot for a small-town boy. I never forgot that lesson and as good as a teacher he repeated this for many years.

Later he took me outside of the guest house, arms over my shoulder and asked about what I wanted to become. I told him I wanted to become an Engineer. I thought he would also like that. But he had a deep look at me and said, "That would be your profession. Do you want to become a good person?".

Later he took us to the canteen. I relished on onion pakoras while an Army officer slipped into the chair and sat down in front of us. He was wearing all his colors and accolades and it was a wonderful sight for me. Grandpa introduced him as Dr. S K Salwan. I little did know that I would keep meeting him for the years to come. Dr. SK Salwan is the founder member of the Integrated Guided Missiles Programme of Defence Research. He has many more achievements attached to his name. This was his earliest idea to introduce me to his colleagues who excelled in their work.

We visited the Golconda Fort, Charminar, and Museum during that trip. Grandpa on the final day asked me which place I liked the most. I said the Musical clock at Salar Jung Museum which performed for the longest at 12:00 PM. I returned from the trip with a small video game gifted by him. After that gift, he continued giving me many gifts. Each gift was better than the other and mostly falls in the category of knowledge.

Grandpa had a grand plan in his mind to introduce me to the greatest people so that their greatness imprinted on me. •

TEACHER

"Teaching is a very noble profession that shapes the character, caliber, and future of an individual. If the people remember me as a good teacher, that will be the biggest honor for me."

- Dr. A. P. J. Abdul Kalam

I entered into an interview waiting hall of Anna University. It was both exhilarating and tension-filled moments. I was waiting for the course selection interview for my Masters at Anna University. I had completed Mechanical Engineering graduation from a small town. The University office staff kept telling me that I was in the top 25 and need not worry. Finally, I sat in front of Dean, Academics of Anna University. He started explaining me about the courses available. I interrupted him. I told him that I want to go to Madras Institute of Technology (MIT) Chrompet. The ideas was to study Manufacturing Engineering. He got puzzled. More lucrative courses were available. Moreover studying at the Guindy campus produced more opportunistic. Little did he know that I wanted to study at MIT for a reason, to further the legacy.

I learned subjects like Nanotechnology, Precision

Engineering, Robotics, and Computer Aided Product Design. My days were going fast. I heard Dr. Abdul Kalam has resigned from his position as Principal Scientific Adviser. He was joining Anna University as a Professor. An invisible hand again brought me close to my Grandpa.

Those days I stayed in Birla hostel where there is a common phone available on every floor. One day in the evening, my senior called out to me saying that someone wants to talk to me. When I picked up, I heard the long hello followed by "Buddy how are you doing?". He told me that he stayed in the new hostel in the 1940s and wanted me to explain in detail about MIT's present environment. My friends and seniors thought I was talking to my Grandfather. But they never realized I was talking to someone who would go onto become the President of India.

During one of those phone conversations, he asked me what do I want? I told him that I want the book 'Word Power Made Easy'. I got it within a week. But after that, he kept on asking whether I completed the book.

I told him that I wanted to meet him with my friends. I told a few of my friends and many didn't believe. Three of them agreed to come for my sake. The Police stopped us at the Ramanujam Centre for Computation. They wanted to take a photo and check the camera to be sure. We entered the room and heard the usual greeting "Hello buddy, How are you?". We had customary introductions and small talk. He then explained about World Knowledge Platform, Providing Urban Amenities in Rural Areas, taking products out of laboratories to reach the market. He told us, "I like teaching". He further said he has devised a course based on the ideas discussed and he would soon teach at MIT .

I learned that day that ideas drive him and the same is the source of his greatness. No matter what position he was in, he believed in ideas and tried to implement them by finding ways.

During one of those phone conversations, he asked me what do I want? I told him that I want the book 'Word Power Made Easy'. I got it within a week. But after that, he kept on asking whether I completed the book. It was his commitment even towards giving a gift. I read the index also so that I remained true to his expectation.

One day there was a notice in the hostel notice board. It said that Dr. Abdul Kalam is giving a lecture at Rajam Hall to 3000 students and it is open for everyone to attend. I silently went and sat in the hall. As usual, he enthralled the students with the presentation, anecdotes, and jokes. He encouraged them to ask questions and answered them powerfully. I myself forgot who he was and felt bitten by his enthusiasm. Then he left to have lunch at the vegetarian mess.

I reached there and my assistant warden was standing outside the mess. Till this time, nobody knew about my connection with him. I told my warden to go and tell Dr. Abdul Kalam that I want to see him. He laughed at me and said everyone is saying similar things. I insisted to please tell Dr. Abdul Kalam that Gulaam wanted to see him. He rushed out after a few minutes and said Dr. Abdul Kalam asked you to come inside immediately.

I went inside. I saw Dr. Abdul Kalam sitting with my Dean, my HOD, and Dr. Mannar Jawahar. Later Dr. Mannar Jawahar became the Vice-Chancellor of Anna University. There were also other important people. He simply said, "Gulaam Sahib, come and have lunch with me". All the top people turned and looked at me. I was a slim young student with spectacles who didn't have any resemblance or connection to Dr. Abdul Kalam. Then Grandpa said, "He is my grandson, actually my brother's grandson".

After lunch, we came out with his hand over my shoulder. Many students were waiting to get a glimpse of him or to get an auto-graph. He sat in the car and said, "Study well, your life depends on it".

My post-graduation project was at National Aerospace Laboratory. The project was design and analysis of a moving part of SARAS civilian aircraft. At that time Grandpa told me,

"You don't have to take aerospace because of me, do only if you like it". I obviously liked it. It involved design and finite element analysis of aircraft propeller mechanism.

Fast-forwarding a few months, I made a presentation, on my final thesis. It went non-stop for two hours in front of the review committee at NAL Propulsion Division. I was able to answer most of the questions. But failed in aerodynamic related questions where my guide Mr. Jayaraman helped out. The review committee has to approve my thesis. Then I can submit it to my University for getting the final degree. "If Dr. Kalam was sitting here, would he approve this project?" asked Dr. Murugesan, HOD of Propulsion Division.

Towards early 2002, I was busy completing my above-mentioned project. I heard on the radio that Dr. Kalam is participating in the election process for the President of India. I was so happy, I tried to call his office to talk to him. I got information that Mr. Atal Bihari Vajpayee has spoken to him a few hours before. He was being visited by Ms. Jayalalitha and Mr. Karunanidhi. I could not get through and I got disappointed. But his office told me to call in the night. I somehow got connected and he came on-line. He said, "Buddy I am very busy. You remain in touch.". I told him how happy I was.

I could not help but think that he left his powerful Government position to become a teacher. But the Universe wanted more of him. He was there teaching only for a short period at Anna University. I felt he came there as if only to teach during the period when I studied. I further thought that it is going to be impossible to meet him after he becomes President of India. The Universe had other plans though. •

MEET THE PRESIDENT Chapter 3

"The Chair should not bring fame to you, you should bring honor to the Chair"

- Dr. A.P.J. Abdul Kalam

It was a cold Bengaluru morning. I was struggling to calculate manually the maximum force acting on a spring-loaded mechanism. This mechanism controls the pitch of the propeller. I took a break. I called my mother. I learned that the whole family is getting ready to attend the Sworning-in ceremony of 11th President of India, Dr. A.P.J. Abdul Kalam. I had to join them at Chennai along with my cousin.

Just a few days before the travel, I contracted a high fever. It stayed on for the next whole week. With that fever, I traveled to Chennai. When I reached the Railway station, I identified a coach full of family. Soon I got lost in talking to them. On the way train stopped at scheduled stations. At each station, my maternal Grandpa met with fans and well-wishers of Dr. Abdul Kalam. They followed traditional garlanding rituals and offered sweets. They were celebrating their most favorite scientist becoming the President of India.

In the heart of those people, the name of Dr. A.P.J. Abdul Kalam, the son of the soil, most respected and leader of common people got etched permanently. I hardly could react, maybe because of my fever.

At 12:00 am during the long train journey to Delhi, one of my relatives woke me up. He said one Hindi news channel wants to interview someone who can speak in Hindi. That was my first TV interview. With fever running high, at 12:00 am, I gave the interview in Hindi (for a Tamilian like me it is comparable to suffering from fever). I managed to answer how happy we were as a family and how we look forward to the sworning-in Ceremony. I didn't answer only one question well. When asked about how our lives are going to change at multiple levels, I asked, "What is going to change?". Maybe I was naive or that was the right answer.

We reached Delhi having similar ceremonies all along the way. A bus took us to an Army area where we were to stay at the DRDO guest house. I never imagined I will frequent this area after many years.

The day before the sworning-in ceremony, Grandpa visited us. My fever was still there. He didn't hear my congratulation.

He was worried that fever was continuing and doctors were not able to identify the reason for the fever. He then sent me to the Institute of Nuclear Medicine and Allied Science (DRDO Lab) to do all kinds of tests on me. When I returned I learned that there is a live show in a top Hindi news channel. I had to take part along with my cousin and Mr. Y S Rajan (YSR).

The most important part of the interview was when the anchor asked me, "What does it mean to you, as your Grandpa becomes President of India?". I told him, "It gives hope to small-town boys and girls. It inspires them to think that they too can become President of India one day".

The Parliament of India stood before me with all mightiness. We entered through a special gate and sat together. We were more than 50 of us eagerly waiting for the ceremony to commence. Dr. L K Advani was there asking me and my cousins about what do we do. We settled into our seats.

It was my first entry into Rashtrapati Bhawan. The size and facilities there amazed me. I have never seen a palace like that in my life before. Long corridors, glimmering lights, armed personnel

Time froze when Grandpa took the oath. Even the clapping seemed to be in slow motion. He then started his speech with **"Endaroo Mahanubhavulu. Andariki Vandanamulu".** It took many moments before the applause settled. He knew how to capture the attention of the people. He went on talking about his big ideas for the nation. I didn't know when the speech ended. I told myself that I have to learn to speak like him one day. I never realized how much preparation went in there. The invisible hand once again wanted to grant my wish.

Later we witnessed the sending off ceremony for President of India Mr. KR Narayanan. It was my first entry into Rashtrapati Bhawan. The size and facilities there amazed me. I have never seen a palace like that in my life before. Long corridors, glimmering lights, armed personnel, Delhi police, uniformed butlers and office people. I felt out of place immediately.

Rashtrapati Bhawan organized a get together for the family. The President of India meets the family after assuming the office. I saw my Grandpa first time in Bandhgala suit. I kept on seeing him like that after that. The 11th President of India didn't appear to have changed much. He asked quickly about my fever. Spiritual representatives from major religions performed prayers one after another. It was a sight to watch. My grandpa offered blessings to his brother.

When I congratulated him on becoming 11th President of India, he told me, "The Chair should not bring fame to you, you should bring honor to the Chair.". You have to raise the level of the position by bringing great ideas to serve this great nation. You have to use the position to do something good for the people of this great Nation".

The ceremony was about to get close and President of India started leaving. Suddenly everyone wanted to take a photo and it was time for a group photo session. YSR asked me to coordinate the arrangement. This was my first interaction with Rashtrapati Bhawan staff. They were too nice to listen to my broken Hindi and arranged the chairs in a quick time. We got a big final family photo. That was my first experience in the logistics of events. This coordination experience would become better part of my life for many years.

Later during the tour of Rashtrapati Bhawan, I remained hypnotized. I cherish those moments when I first visited the Museum, Mughal gardens, Ashoka Hall, President's study (President's office room) and family wing. We took photos everywhere. I roamed and consumed the beauty of the place like it was last time. Once again, I was wrong. ●

STATESMAN

"This place is like a University. You will meet a lot of people. You can use it to learn as much you can"

- Dr. A.P.J. Abdul Kalam

In early 2003, I successfully completed my Masters in Engineering from MIT, Chrompet, Chennai. I blew up a good chance to get into one of India's top IT services companies even after I reached the final human resources interview. Two of my classmates embraced the opportunity and went on to reach the USA. I wanted to be in the technology field and that too related to mechanical engineering. But one does not always get what they wish for.

When I reached a desperate state to settle in a job, YSR made a reference to Mr. Tarun Das of Confederation of Indian Industry (CII). I had no idea what I was getting into. I got a call for an interview at Chennai. I met the Head of Energy services and post the interview, CII felt that I would fit in one of their Technology Development and Promotion Centers. I had a few more rounds of telephonic interviews. I then got an offer to join APTDC (Andhra Pradesh Technology Development and

Promotion Centre) at Hyderabad. But the invisible hand would have its way, my reporting manager got transferred to New Delhi. When he asked me whether I would come to Delhi to work with him at the Technology Division of CII, I replied in affirmative without thinking much.

In August 2003, I reached Delhi with my family. Obviously, we had one family member in New Delhi and we had to stay with him. Once again, I entered the Rashtrapati Bhawan. This time Grandpa had already settled in the role of 11th President of India. I met once again a very charismatic leader transformed completed for the role as it required. I enjoyed the luxury for some time.

The day before the first day of my work, we had a meeting at Rashtrapati Bhawan. Grandpa along with YSR was ready with a lot of questions. Whether I knew about my work and was I ready to do it to perfection and many more. After grilling me for some time and making me further afraid, he wanted to put me at ease. He asked me about my hobbies. I said cricket and amateur signing. So he asked for a song. Of all the songs I knew nothing came to my mind. I did not imagine I would get President of India as the audience to display my amateur singing talent. I finally chose "Ninnai Saranadaindhen" by

Mahakavi Bharathiyar. I had some practice listening to tapes. I delivered in a feeble and trembling voice. Surprisingly he liked the delivery but expected a youthful song from me.

I did not look confident in front of his eyes. So he took me for a walk through Mughal Garden. He tried to instill confidence in me. He talked about how he lost all hope when he did not get selected as a Pilot. He returned to do something in service of the country and it all went well. I felt over 75 years of life condensed in a few sentences doesn't look like a struggle. But I was still afraid.

We were strolling through Mughal Gardens. I was not even in the mood of looking at the beautiful flowers. After playing with a deep thought he told me, "You should not get defeated by the problems. You should become the Captain and defeat the problems".

At that moment I did not feel like properly going to work. The car raced through the traffic and those who knew about those cars gave way. I eventually reached at 8:00 am and started waiting at the CII office to join my first day of job.

The next day I had to reach Gurgaon by 9:00 am. But Grandpa made sure I started from Rashtrapati Bhawan at 730 am. I traveled in a black car reserved for family members with security sitting in the front. At that moment I did not feel like properly going to work. The car raced through the traffic and those who knew about those cars gave way. I eventually reached at 8:00 am and started waiting at the CII office to join my first day of job.

While I was settling on the job, there was some commotion at the reception area. One of my colleagues told me that the security urgently wanted to speak to me. I got to know from the security that my black car was parked in the reserved parking of Mr. Tarun Das, the Director General of CII. I had to move down to the parking to make them go away. How could I have explained to them that an employee joined that very day could not park in the space of CEO. But the car waited for me till evening as that was their orders.

I returned in the evening to Rashtrapati Bhawan. My parents already were gone back home. I felt alone in that big palace. The ever-smiling Rashtrapati Bhawan staff kept asking me about my needs. They were too impressed to see the only family member staying there. Once again Grandpa came to

the rescue. I got introduced to various officers in the President of India's office.

Grandpa took me again for a walk in the Mughal Gardens. This time I was able to see the row of roses. He even mentioned the name of a few varieties. He asked me a question which was far lethal than his missiles. The question was, "What did you do today?". When I explained he was not satisfied. He told me, "If your goal is to serve the industry and in turn our country then what did you do today to achieve that goal?". I was silent as I didn't have any answers. But he asked this question again and again to me till he chose to rest himself at Rameswaram.

We discussed a lot of things, including his idea for improving the Mughal Gardens. Finally, he asked me whether I was happy staying in Rashtrapati Bhawan. I was never used to such luxury so I didn't say anything. He asked me whether I wanted to stay outside. It was a wonderful proposition for me, to experience freedom. The same day I moved to Brahmos Guest House in Vasant Vihar. Dr. Sivathanu Pillai, CEO of Brahmos, a colleague of Grandpa was happy to have me.

I had all set up at the Guest House for a few months before I found my rented house. The next day free of the black car, I traveled on the local bus to the office. It was liberating and felt normal. I started thinking of buying a vehicle or finding regular transport to the office.

As the days went by, I could hardly stay in the Guest House. Dr. Pillai came to visit me in the evening to check on me. I told him that I want to find my house immediately. He put one of his able colleagues on the job to get a rented house at Munirka.

I got to meet Grandpa once I settled in the rented house where I joined few guys who worked in the IT (Information Technology) industry. Grandpa asked me whether I have settled in the house and was happy. I was more than happy. I had my freedom and my own chance to experience life. I hardly mentioned about my self and my Grandpa to anyone. That saved me from a lot of trouble.

He then told me to concentrate on work but I was free to call him and also to visit him whenever I wanted. He also told me, "Rashtrapati Bhawan means different ideas to different people. For me, this is place of work. This place is like an University for you. You will meet lot of people. You can use it to learn as much you can".

He stood by his words and introduced many great people of this country to me. He made sure I considered Rashtrapati Bhawan like a University. The place did provide opportunities to learn and improve my knowledge. •

GRANDPA, THE GREATEST

"You have a page in the book of human history. Fill that page with your dreams and actions. That page may be a very important page in the book of human history."

- Dr. A.P.J. Abdul Kalam

I really do not remember when my regular visits to Rashtrapati Bhawan started. I had a routine and by that time I knew I got used to it. Every Friday night I used to travel by office cab and get down at Teen Murti. A black car comes and takes me inside. I used to get settled in one of the guest rooms. The first time I remember, Grandpa called me to a meeting room called TI room. When I entered I saw some of the brightest brains of the country inside that room working on something.

Grandpa quickly assigned me to Dr. Pillai. He said, "You both guys come out with one-pager on this subject.", and left. I sat on the computer and opened a word processor. I thought it is going to be a cakewalk. But as wise Dr. Pillai was, he asked me to first work on an outline before typing it out. We decided on an outline and the next step was to find the sources of such information. Once we identified sources of information, I had to use both primary and secondary research methods to collect the information. Grandpa returned and uttered his usual trademark remark, "You have done nothing."

It was time for lunch. It was my first time to have lunch at 6:30 pm. I planned to eat a little bit and skip dinner. But lunch was again more of a discussion on many ideas. Grandpa used to discuss in such lunch meetings a lot of things. I was not supposed to hear. I have maintained such a stance until now. I never asked about the things discussed with some big people however juicy it was. It was like having a bar of chocolate in front of you and not eating it.

The lunch used to be always simple. Dosa with chutney followed by curd rice. Once I started going, the staff added more items to the lunch. I used to eat Dosa without sambhar. Grandpa used to tell his staff, "Give some gravy for this dry fellow." One side the staff didn't want to

I used to eat Dosa without sambhar. Grandpa used to tell his staff, "Give some gravy for this dry fellow." One side the staff didn't want to annoy me but had to follow the President of India's orders. So I had to eat sambhar soaked dosas annoy me but had to follow the President of India's orders. So I had to eat sambhar soaked dosas in the name of Mr. President. One more interesting stuff he used to give is bitter gourd chips. He used to intently look at the face to see any expression change after eating the bitter stuff. I was good at hiding my expression and he remained disappointed for some time until he found a much bitter one.

After lunch, he immediately asked us to continue the work. I finished the one-pager as advised by Dr. Pillai and he left. Grandpa came in around 9:00 PM and asked whether I verified all the data with the concerned institutions. I found out that we had to check with a Vice-Chancellor of a Central University. Maj. Gen. Swaminathan, Officer on Special Duty with President of India, decided to call the Vice-Chancellor at 10:00 pm. The Vice-Chancellor told us that the information is available in his office and he would go to his office and send it. We received the information by 11:00 pm. By 12:00 am we were ready with a version of the speech Grandpa was to deliver. With three different teams, involving inputs from top people, the first version of the speech looked solid.

Grandpa saw the version and simply blew it away. He looked at me and said, "Look at this fellow, it is only 12:00 AM and he is feeling sleepy and hungry." He announced Dinner at 12:30

AM. It was again a simple dinner. I dragged myself through the dinner and was ready to crash into the bed. At 2:00 AM, he told me, "How are you going to sleep immediately after eating, let's go for a walk." This is how our late night walks started. We entered Mughal Gardens and walked till 3:30 AM. He came to my room and looked inside. The first remark was, "Buddy your room is bigger than mine!"

By the time we finished that speech, it had gone into more than 35 versions. I didn't understand why it took so much effort to assemble that speech. I asked him about that. Grandpa explained to me that one should have a goal every 5 years in life. That goal should be about how many people one could touch and change their lives. He also said it doesn't matter whether you are a big or small guy and in power or not. We can always make a change in others' lives. He wanted to use his current position as President of India to inspire the youngsters of the country. He was talking to the future leaders of this great nation. He had a goal of meeting one million students/ youngsters in his life. He told me with a serious face, "You should have a goal in your life. There are many people in India below poverty line. Would you be able to touch and change their lives? You have a page in the book of human history. Fill that page with your dreams and actions. That page may be a very important page in the book of human history." So he believed inspiring a youngster is a serious job and he wanted to put some serious effort into that. His speeches were the medium of reaching the youngsters of India and inspiring them.

I realized his greatness when we were working on one such speech. He was preparing for his speech on the 60th Independence Day. His office has already developed few versions but he wanted more punch. My opinion was that the citizens of the country had to rethink about their duties whatever profession they were in. The idea was to emphasize among the citizens to think of India as their country. To further encourage them to excel in performing their basic duties like tax payments, waste management, teaching, and social inclusion. Grandpa agreed on this idea but felt that it was not enough to complete the speech. When I saw the few versions down he had sprinkled those ideas in the speech. The speech needed a powerful topic. There were many ideas and longer titles but he told me to think of something which was short and powerful.

I took a day and told him my topic was "National Awakening". He asked me to explain why that should be the topic. I told him that the citizens are aware of their duties. They are just thinking that one person can not change anything. But millions of them doing a small change would change the course of the country. The nation has to be awakened again to the new challenges in front of her. Grandpa made me defend this in front of his expert team. I miserably failed to make an impression. As a fair leader, he chose a popular topic for the speech.

On the day of the speech, I was following the speech in TV and online. The topic was promptly displayed on the website as "National Awakening". Grandpa later told me many liked the topic and line of thinking. A septuagenarian and first citizen of India to listen and accept ideas from the small-town man in 20s certainly showed his greatness in abundance.

I never realized how many months had passed while I was working with him on many such ideas. I was comfortably settled in Munirka in South West Delhi in a single room. Grandpa gifted me with a laptop and printer to get me involved more in the work. When his staff came to deliver the printer to my single room, they were surprised to see someone from the President's family living like that. But I had already seen someone great living in a room smaller than mine. •

TASK MASTER Chapter 6

"Look at your Grandfather, follow him on practicing discipline"

- Dr. A.P.J. Abdul Kalam

Grandpa was very particular on matters of discipline. Though he doesn't look to be strict with his ever-smiling face, he made sure I followed all protocols. As soon as I settled into a rhythm visiting Rashtrapati Bhawan, he wanted to set some rules for me on spending time there. After going for late night/ early morning walks with him, he directed me to the gym at 06:30 am in the morning. I used to sleepwalk all the way to the gym and exercise on the treadmill with rapid blinking eyes.

Grandpa's keen eye for discipline comes from his father and his brother (my grandfather). My maternal grandfather followed a strict regime in his life for many many years. Now he has surpassed 100 years it is worth to mention what kept him healthy. He used to get up at 4:00 am, offer prayer, recite the Holy Quran and out for the coconut garden by 6:00 am. He walked for more than 10 kilometers every day for many years. The diet was nutritious home-made food. On holidays, he would also take us to the garden early in the morning.

Grandpa as always added more items to the already strict regime. This was the time I got introduced to some of the friends of Grandpa. There used to be Golf sessions at the Golf course at Rashtrapati Bhawan. I have only seen Golf on the TV. Bajaj Uncle assumed the role of my coach. I was first digging yorkers from my toes like while playing cricket. I tried to unlearn cricketing habits and it was very difficult. Grandpa told me that the brain gets activated once for unlearning and another time while learning new skills such as Golf. That was his intention.

Grandpa never missed a chance to infuse humor into daily life. He believed humor keeps the human spirit at high levels of performance. I remember a day once he went missing from his room. I was waiting downstairs to accompany him to go to attend a function. Generally, ADC[1] brings him from the room.

He walked for more than 10 kilometers every day for many years. The diet was nutritious home-made food. On holidays, he would also take us to the garden early in the morning.

[1] *Aide-de-Camp shortly called ADC are officers from Army, Navy and Air Force serving the President of India on various duties including providing security.*

Suddenly I heard increased traffic in the walkie talkie. ADC was running from first floor to ground floor searching for Grandpa. He was not in his room. Delhi Police in the premise was alerted. They also started searching. I got tense and I went on searching from floor to floor. After sometime Grandpa was standing with us appeared out of nowhere. He told the ADC that he just took a wrong turn. Though the situation was serious, he laughed his heart out. He said," At least you all had good exercise today." Till now it is a mystery whether he genuinely got lost or pulled a prank on us.

The very late night dinners by this time had become a routine. But I could never let my guard down. He used these sessions to inquire about family members. I used to keep small notes as he might ask anything about anyone. On one of the occasions, a relative in the family told him about her interest in a particular subject. He followed up with me about her education and whether her aspirations were the same over a period of time. It is important to remind that he was the President of India. I had to keep notes while he just remembered everything. Even social interactions were projects for him. I was the project manager and he was the Mission Director.

During these Dinner sessions, he used to read a lot of material. One of those is the Intelligence Bureau (IB) reports. I begged him to show me at least a page that is noncontroversial. He answered one day, "Buddy you get all these from media much faster than me". Though it might not be true, it was his way of saying someone to forget it. Then towards the end of one of the Dinner sessions, his assistant brought some certificate to sign for Gallantry Award winners. We were already sleepy. But then he asked how many certificates for which he didn't get an answer. Because there were 200 certificates to sign. He has already been awake for 20 hours and he gets drifted into sleep. His assistant and I had a deal to keep him signing. Whenever he drifted into sleep, I had to cough while I myself was fighting to keep awake. Then one sudden moment Grandpa got very fresh. He started asking who was getting the award and for what purpose. It would become a proper briefing session then on.

Grandpa kept me in check with a walk around Mughal Gardens after most of the meals. On some occasions, there were no rules for the walking exercise. One dark early winter we were walking in the Gardens. It was already 1:00 am and he was talking something serious about family matters. As the

bushes were dark and thick we could never see the army soldier standing guard behind them. Once we took a turn, suddenly the soldier snapped to attention and saluted him. We were little startled by sudden action in the night. But from then on Grandpa started playing a game. At every turn, he used to bet with me if there was a soldier. If he won, I had to taste the most bitter fruit he found for me. He won hands down as usual and I lost. He fondly plucked few small oranges and handed over to me. It was the most bitter thing I ever tasted. He also tasted it but never showed any signs of distaste in his face. He used to offer that orange to relatives and his friends for tasting. He humored them by explaining it was a special fruit from Rashtrapati Bhawan.

For Grandpa every single item is a project of importance. A Musical Fountain was being installed at Rashtrapati Bhawan. One day he took me and asked the responsible staff to show me how it worked. It was full of music, dance of water fountain and colors. I really loved the way it was set up and he also explained how it was designed to conserve water also. After a few weeks he asked just like that," Did you review the progress of the Musical Fountain?" I was stumped as usual. According to him I was in a way responsible for the project. But able people were working and reporting to him on the progress. From then on, I used to go and see the progress, have a test show with different types of music and so on. I reported to him on this for sometime till he felt I did a proper job. Though I could say I had the Musical Fountain all by myself for me to enjoy, I had to report on what I saw as the progress.

As I grew closer with him, Grandpa had further plans to expand my knowledge. •

ENTHUSIASTIC LEADER

Chapter 7

> "When God is with me who can be against"
> *- Dr. A.P.J. Abdul Kalam*

Grandpa's enthusiasm was very contagious and it caught up with everyone around him. Once he became President he started traveling a lot. He used these visits to reach and interact with the young Indians of this country. He wanted to motivate and inspire them to work for the country. But after coming back from a huge tour he still would spend time with me as if nothing happened. He was around 75 years at that time but never showed any signs of tiredness, especially while talking to me.

During those days I mentioned to him that I had to go to my best friend's wedding in Chennai but could not do so due to work. He saw me sad and asked me whether I would like to join him for the tour of Chennai. I didn't realize at that time what was it like to be part of the official tour of President of India. I also underestimated the experience, while traveling with Grandpa officially.

One Sunday evening we departed from Delhi to Chennai. I had to sit in the car at least 30 minutes earlier. The convoy of cars was parked in line and every one of us had a designated car. The convoy started moving like a snake with high speed and precision and we reached the airport. We got escorted through a separate entrance and I got down to see the plane. This is a special plane but not dedicated to the service of the President of India. If it flies President of India I learned that the call sign is Air India One. Indian Air Force operated the flight.

I learned from the staff that I could get snacks, food, and drinks while traveling. They also advised having some sleep as after getting down there would be no time for rest. As soon as we took off, ADC told me that Grandpa was calling me. I entered a room sort of chamber in the flight specially designed for VIPs. Grandpa was sitting and eagerly inviting me inside. He told his secretary to give me the speech copy

At one point I had to tell him that he has to slow down. I asked time for his staff to eat otherwise they were all going hungry moving from one place to another. He smiled and picked up a plate to eat curd rice.

for the 150th year Celebration of the University of Madras. I understood that all my dream of traveling with pleasure in Air India One was over.

I was sincerely reading the speech and writing my input on a separate notepad. At that moment, I saw men in Air Force uniform enter the chamber. They saluted and briefed Grandpa on the weather, flight details, and time of flight. As President of India is the Commander-in-Chief, the Air Force briefs his during the flight. Even with all those things happening, Grandpa introduced me to the Captain. Finally, when I finished my inputs giving session, Grandpa offered a simple dinner. He then let me go. When I sat down in my seat we were already descending into Chennai. Till then I had never traveled on a Helicopter and I was looking forward to it.

While we were getting down Grandpa's secretary told me to look for a car in my name and immediately get into it. I learned otherwise it was difficult to get back in the convoy. We reached Raj Bhawan and a simple dinner was in order. Grandpa among his friends then started talking about finding a suitable girl for me to marry. There were already people waiting to meet him and this session generally would go on after midnight. I got relieved as I was to stay in a Hotel. They told me that I am a State Guest and got treated like one. While I was leaving Grandpa asked me to work with his team member Mr. Ponraj for the next day's arrangement.

We were at the University of Madras auditorium till midnight to check on all arrangements. By the time we returned to the Hotel, I truly felt like a Guest of State because of the hard work. I hardly had slept for a few hours. Next I remember, I was sitting at the University of Madras Auditorium, listening to dignitaries on the dais. Just before the National Anthem one of the staff gave me an important tip. After the National Anthem plays, I have to move faster to my car. I knew Grandpa moved very fast. I later realized that I had to use all my athletic skills to reach my car as it was parked long way ahead in the convoy. This way Grandpa kept me fit during the official tours also. During the same trip, there was Presentation of Tholkappiar Award to the then Chief Minister of Tamil Nadu, Dr M Karunanidhi. Grandpa took serious note for my love of Tamil and wanted me to be part of this program. In those few hours we heard lot of Tamil speeches touching the ears and some touching the heart. Grandpa was well prepared with a speech with both Tamil and English combined. He appreciated

Dr. Karunanidhi and one particular line was much appreciated by audience. That line translates in English as "Kalaignar is delivering such masterpieces in Tamil and I don't know which ink he uses in his pen". It was obvious he stole the applause of the audience for many minutes.

Grandpa wanted to give me an experience of a lifetime. He offered me to be part of the next official trip where he planned to go to Rameswaram also. He told me it was just two states Kerala and Tamil Nadu. The trip had 22 programs and he dashed through them one after another with childlike enthusiasm. He created history by delivering that many speeches, on different subjects, over the next few days. I traveled with him on Air India One, Helicopters, cars in the convoy, boat and little bit of walking. I got tired but he never showed any sign of tiredness. At one point I had to tell him that he has to slow down. I asked time for his staff to eat otherwise they were all going hungry moving from one place to another. He smiled and picked up a plate to eat curd rice.

One more trip where he showed a lot of interest was to take me to Puttaparthi. Grandpa was invited to inaugurate the Sri Sathya Sai International Centre for sports among others. During the program, Grandpa sent a word for me to reach the stage. He quietly introduced me to Sri Satya Sai Baba himself. I had no question or any comments, so I simply said Good Morning. Sri Satya Sai Baba smiled and held my hands for a few more seconds before releasing me with an even bigger smile. This was the trip when convoy left me and Dr. YS Rajan at a Guest House. Because Dr. Rajan was there he managed to get me on track otherwise it was one of the horrific moments.

There are many such memorable moments on traveling with him. In Ooty, we were getting out after his speech. Already security forces were very worried because of the terrain they had to guard. There were a lot of his fans on the roads. We were moving slowly in the car and at one turn there were a lot of school students standing and waving at him. He stopped the car and got down. He approached the students and shook hands with them. He answered questions, signed autographs while the police were too worried about protecting him. Another memorable trip was to Haridwar in Uttarakhand. Air Force personnel in-charge was not ready to fly the helicopter due to bad weather. Grandpa asked how many people are waiting and from how long they were waiting. On learning this he simply said we had to go. It was one of those joy rides going up and down in the wind and turbulence with difficult visibility. But finally we reached and Grandpa once again received a standing ovation.

When I asked about such incidents that how he was not worried about that too much, he answered, "When God is with me who can be against".

Grandpa's wish for taking me to an international trip did not materialize. He was all enthusiastic to take me on a trip where he was addressing the European Parliament. Every now and then the speech resurfaces on social media. He gets a standing ovation from the members of European Parliament. I was ready and my travel documents were being processed. At the last moment, one genius colleague convinced Grandpa that I would add no value to the trip and he would. He also set a tone that if family members go on international trip then there would be media frenzy. I told Grandpa that I was willing to go on the trip without taking any benefits. But still he was worried that I would end up in a controversy. I wish I could have gone to witness that historic speech.   •

THE PERFECT HOST

"If you do good it would always come back to you and same is the case with doing something bad".

- Dr. A.P.J. Abdul Kalam

Grandpa played a perfect host almost all the time. Whenever there was a Head of State visited Rashtrapati Bhawan he used to ask me if I wanted to attend the Banquet Dinner. I was never keen. He liked our quite dinner eating Dosas. I asked him once how he played host without the first lady. He answered that intelligent conversation filled up the space. He thoroughly impressed the then US President George W Bush, with a presentation on Energy Independence. The same effect he had on Pakistan President Musharraf when he spoke on length about his dream of Providing Urban Amenities in Rural Areas (PURA). I got to see the presentations and his ruminations but could not meet the Presidents.

He made sure that his office invited me for all At-home functions and other functions he hosted. I skipped many just because I didn't know what to do out there. I enjoyed the company of his friends who are also scientists. But one such function was very memorable. I was among large gathering doing my duty as Host on behalf of Grandpa. Suddenly I heard a lot of people searching for me. Grandpa was calling. I saw from the distance he was among the most powerful people. As usual I was hesitant. But he quickly waved his hand and asked me to come fast.

I saw five of the Prime Ministers of India sitting in a row. AB Vajpayee was sitting in the middle with I K Gujral, VP Singh, and others flanking him. He introduced me as his Grandson for which everyone looked at me with much amusement. As I didn't expect this to happen I just said that I was very happy to meet them all and left. Later I realized what a great opportunity it was to meet the top-most architects of this country. That too I got introduced by the President of India. Grandpa later told me that his intention was to inspire

Grandpa asked me to write a piece on my experience attending the concert of Ustad Bismillah Khan. He made me write an experimental style. The write up is given in the section Demo of Love.

me to grow up to someone like the Prime Ministers.

I never understood the true depth of his love for art. My first experience was when Grandpa asked me to attend Aamir Raza Husain's, 'The Legend of Ram' (based on Ramayana). I also didn't know that it was going to be a very embarrassing moment. On the day of the play when I got into the designated car, two attendants from the house also got into the car. I thought they were coming because there was free space in my car. The play was a very nice production with great professionalism in acting. I saw Grandpa was enjoying it from a distance.

There was a break during the play. Suddenly the two attendants were standing by my side with huge bags. There was no arrangement for refreshments during the play. The attendants had thoughtfully brought snacks, tea, and water for me. What was embarrassing was the others, seated near me didn't have a chance of getting something to eat. When I got upset, the attendants told me they are used to serving family members of Presidents during such events. I quickly asked them to get back to their seats.

When we returned to the house, Grandpa asked me whether I

learned something from the play. It was based on Ramayana and it has a lot of teachings. After the play, he said that "If you do good it would always come back to you and same is the case with doing something bad".

The most memorable performance was the Jugalbandi Concert by Shehnai Maestro Ustad Bismillah Khan[2]. The stage was set in the lawns of Rashtrapati Bhawan. Unusually there was a large number of guests confirmed for this performance. When the Maestro started with his Shehnai there was no stopping. I had never heard such a piece of music anywhere. For the uninitiated like me in music, it touched my heart and soul and melted me inside. I told

[2] *Grandpa asked me to write a piece on my experience attending the concert of Ustad Bismillah Khan. He made me write an experimental style. The write up is given in the section Demo of Love.*

Grandpa later that the Maestro is blowing part of his life into the Shehnai. That was why it was touching our soul. With a deep thought, he told me, "See what devotion and passion in art can do to you".

There were lot many such performances during his tenure. It touched Odissi, Kathakali, and instruments like Santoor. But there was one performance which I loved because Grandpa took part in it. A musical extravaganza by the Artistes of Shradha U. Shrinivas (Mandolin), Shankar Mahadevan (vocal), Loy Mendonsa (Keyboard), Shivamani (drums) was again planned in the lawns. It was one of the heart-stealing performances. Master Shivamani, as usual, stole the show with his veracity in playing percussion. Towards the end, Grandpa went up to them and started thanking them. At that moment Master Shivamani gave him one of his sticks. They both played a jugalbandhi and made a unique piece of music out of it. I still remember the childish smile on Grandpa's face after he got down from the stage.

Grandpa did a lot of makeover at Rashtrapati Bhawan during his tenure. He installed two huts which he fondly called Thinking Hut and Immortal Hut. He told me that the inspiration for his book Indomitable Spirit came while sitting in this Thinking hut. The huts were made of natural materials and constantly encouraged me to go and sit and think. I did write about some musings inspired from there which Grandpa always appreciated. But sitting in the Immortal Hut also made me anxious thinking about what would I contribute to this society and country.

Grandpa went on to develop a Herbal Garden which attracted many. He later developed the Garden of Senses which appealed to vision, smell and taste. To include visually challenged, he included Braille boards explaining about the plants. He converted the Deer park into biodiversity park and added more inhabitants. According to him, his personal staff who were supposed to serve had now more meaningful work.

During one of our regular visits, he entered the biodiversity park. The caretaker was busy tending to a deer and he didn't look around. The police were trying to get his attention. Grandpa dismissed them and approached the caretaker. The caretaker was astonished to see President standing next to him. Grandpa asked about the animals and thanked him. The Caretaker fell on the feet of Grandpa and told him he is honored that President of India Dr. Abdul Kalam went to him and enquired about his welfare. When I teased him about this he said, "I don't know why that funny guy behaved like that". •

THE TRUE TECHNOCRAT

"Any technology has to result in benefit for common man and society, that is what you have to work for",

- Dr. A.P.J. Abdul Kalam.

Nanotechnology got attached to me during a large part of my work at the Confederation of Indian Industry (CII). In fact when I joined the technology division I handled Nanotechnology and Hydrogen energy to start with. Later on, Robotics got added to the list of technology areas I would handle. When I was studying Masters at Madras Institute of Technology, I was very attracted to Precision engineering and Nanotechnology. Industrial Robots also excited me further. So when the interest areas matched the area of work it kicked off a meaningful career in that direction. I networked and learned from professionals, scientists, and industrialists working on those areas. The interesting fact was that they knew more than me at any point in time.

Nanotechnology, the science of small things, where material got manipulated at the atomic level resulting in amazing properties. It is an interesting subject to deal with. When I first mentioned to Grandpa that I am working with industry and institutes on Nanotechnology, he spent thirty minutes to explain his views on nanotechnology. This was the time when Grandpa decided to make Rashtrapati Bhawan as a focal point of knowledge and learning. He had already organized two meetings one for Bio-fuel and another for nanotechnology at Rashtrapati Bhawan. Later I would get a lot of books from his collection on Nanotechnology and Hydrogen energy.

The way Grandpa explained his vision for bringing any new technology into the country definitely played a role in how I planned and delivered my work. As a first step, he said that I should know the researchers in India in the field of nanotechnology. Fortunately, we won a project from Department of Industrial Policy and Research (DSIR), Govt of India for doing a survey of the status of research in institutes

He happily agreed to speak at the Agro Tech conference to popularize and inspire research institutes and industry to work on such technologies

and industry and compare it with major countries. I had just returned from my maiden air flight to Bangalore where Department of Industrial Policy and Promotion (DIPP), Govt of India and Central Manufacturing Technology Institute (CMTI) had organized a meeting on Nanotechnology. I had met most of the important people in the field, including Dr. S Ahmad who was happy to have me around. He had wealth of experience in research and management and tons of assignment with him but still found a soft corner for a young man.

The second step was to bring our researchers in same the platform with international researchers along with the industry. For this Indo -US S&T Forum ably led by Dr. Arabinda Mitra agreed to support the first-ever Nanotechnology Conclave organized by CII. We got confirmation from a combination of researchers, industry experts, and venture capitalists to attend the conclave. We needed a jewel in the crown moment to make it big and to be noticed by policymakers and industry. When I told this to Grandpa he agreed to Inaugurate the Conclave. He told me that CII has to approach him officially. Then the official machinery went into action. Grandpa officially agreed after the Secretary, DST Dr. V S Ramamurthy met him and explained the need for such a Conclave.

This was my first ever experience of organizing a conference independently. My head was already spinning with the President's security as one added element contributing to it. One day I was sitting opposite to President's ADC reviewing security for the Conclave. This was one different experience where the ADC to act professionally but at the same time had a family member handling the event. But the rest of the CII team made it easy for him by providing all the details. They were seasoned in handling VVIP security over the years.

On the day of the Conclave, the then Director General, Mr. N Srinivasan (he passed away recently) asked staff members of CII also to attend the event. It so happened I had to pass on some information to President's ADC sitting on the dais behind Grandpa. When I walked to him, Grandpa called me and asked me what was the matter. The cameras captured closely and enough people got to know that President of India Dr. Abdul Kalam is speaking to some guy in CII. Grandpa made sure he spoke to me for a few minutes so that enough people noticed. That is how subtle he blessed me on occasions.

In the evening of the Conclave, he called me and said the next step is to create avenues for international collaborative

Research & Development (R&D) in Nanotechnology area. He also asked me to distribute his speech to the participants. This further guided me to work within CII on International Industrial R&D Funds and contributing to the team which established the organization Global Innovation and Technology Alliance (GITA). This organization coordinates Industrial R&D funds with handful of nations on multiple sectors and areas.

As time went by, I had brought scientists and experts from the USA, United Kingdom, Japan, Canada, South Korea, and Russia on nanotechnology to India to forge collaborations. I had done this over a period of 10 years. Grandpa asked me a question, "What was your vision when you started working in this area?" I told him that I wanted to start a translational research center where the institute and industry could work on nanotechnology. Grandpa said this is the time to go for setting up a pilot center to start showing some products. I was very apprehensive considering the amount of investment required. Even the big nations of the world were yet to have any success.

CII with its strength proposed to the Government of Gujarat to set up a Centre of Excellence in Nanotechnology under the Vibrant Gujarat Investment Program. The then industry

secretary Mr. M Sahu told me to convince him with three slides on why he should fund the center. I had to do it. I had no idea if he was already convinced with the proposal and the show of strength from CII. But he agreed to set up such a center. Dr. S Ahmad helped to set up a small facility initially to work on Green Chemistry based products. The first research idea was to work on organic nano dyes for fabrics. Grandpa told me what you wrote ten years ago in a piece of document has now become a reality. The Centre did not stand the test of time as it was too early for such an initiative.

Grandpa inspired throughout my professional life as I moved on from one assignment to another. When I handled a joint venture organisation of CII and Govt. of Tamil Nadu, Agro Food processing and Automotive were the areas where R&D collaborations were required. He happily agreed to speak at the Agro Tech conference to popularize and inspire research institutes and industry to work on such technologies.

Grandpa shared new technologies he comes across and tried to see if I could bring the industrial element into it. Areas like Assistive technologies, where Robots could be used to help differently-abled and elderly was his interest. Starting from Solar cells to Hyper-plane the discussions never ended when we talked about technology. But even though the discussions were very serious there was always a funny guy hiding in him.   •

THE FUNNY GUY Chapter 10

"It is much easier to understand rocket science than marriage."

- Dr. A.P.J. Abdul Kalam

Grandpa was a big source of humor all the time. Whether it was 2:00 am in the morning or under a scorching sun, it doesn't matter. He is known to say things that brought smiles around. His all-time famous one-liner is "Where is the funny guy?". And whenever someone praised him he responded most of the time with "You are a funny guy, I say".

One of the incidents worth mentioning is when I went with him to the mosque inside Rashtrapati Bhawan. Grandpa had his designated place in the car sitting on the left and I sit on the right. When we were about to enter the mosque he told me to remove the shoes and keep them in the car. He made sure that day I also received all kinds of honors bestowed on him at the mosque. I humbly accepted for the sake of Grandpa. When we were finished we returned to the car. As per protocol, they had turned the car to face the way forward and Grandpa was supposed to sit on the right side. When we got in the car first we looked for our shoes. To our surprise, the shoes had changed places. He never liked someone touching his shoes or changing its place. So the next time when we went to the mosque we ourselves changed the position of the shoes. We returned to the car with more surprises. This time they had not turned around the car as we had to go somewhere else from there. When we got in the car the shoes, as usual, were in the right places. Grandpa ended it with the words "Funny guys".

One of the moments in his life where he had all the fun was when my mother told him that it was time to get me married. He always kept his ideas to himself and later revealed in a setting which made it funnier. Grandpa had some relatives in Sri Lanka. Obviously, in some way, they are my relatives as well. They had approached him and wanted to visit him at the Rashtrapati Bhawan. He told me well in advance to be there on that day and play host. Grandpa took me to his room. With a beautiful smile on his face, he asked me, "Did you like any of the young girls? They are all well educated and settled in Sri Lanka." His whole idea of me hosting the relatives was to look for a match for me.

I promptly was standing in front of him at the Study, the official working room of Grandpa. He got a call from his assistants that the relatives have arrived. Out came a response "What relatives?". He further told his assistant that he was not aware of any relatives visiting that day. Now I got a call from his assistant on my mobile for which Grandpa asked me not to answer. He wanted his assistant to sweat it out and it was his way of playing a prank.

Finally, he yielded and sent me to receive the guests. There were about fifteen people representing different age groups. I made them sit at the lawns in a semi-circle as decided earlier. Grandpa came in and introduced me around. I saw in the corner of the eye his assistant running towards the lawn to handle the situation and taking a breath when he found Grandpa was there. When all the relatives bid adieu, Grandpa took me to his room. With a beautiful smile on his face, he asked me, "Did you like any of the young girls? They are all well educated and settled in Sri Lanka." His whole idea of me hosting the relatives was to look for a match for me. This was an opportunity to make fun of me.

Grandpa also played matchmaker on one another occasion. He took me on an official tour to Ambur University. He tirelessly gave degrees to hundreds of students. My biggest embarrassment was when he later told the Vice-Chancellor "We are looking for a suitable bride for him." After returning he told in front of his colleagues, "I gave you an opportunity in Ambur you didn't use it". This was one more opportunity for humor. Everyone knew if I was not serious with the work during the visits he never liked it. Fun and humor was his part to play.

The funny part of his side remained all through his life. For example, he never celebrated his birthdays at a station. He always planned to be traveling so that no serious effort is taken to celebrate his birthday. I generally call him on his birthday and would not know what to tell him. He liked my problem and I generally end up saying that it was his birthday. He answered by saying how many times he has taken orbit around the sun and ended with wishing me all the best. So I used to tell him that Air India celebrated most of his birthdays than his friends or family.

He also made sure he traveled when there is an event hosted at Delhi that he had to attend. He skipped all Dinners and at-home functions. He wanted to dedicate his time to students and inspire citizens. He wanted to use this time to discuss his innovations and ideas. Only once when President Obama came to India he had to attend. I later asked him "First time standing in a queue to meet someone?". He just replied, "You are a funny guy". •

THE SUPER SPIRIT Chapter 11

"Religion must graduate into spirituality and unify the minds of people towards the cause of national development. "

- Dr. A.P.J. Abdul Kalam.

Grandpa is truly a super spirit. I could experience his spirituality as I spend long hours with him talking about religion, God, compassion, love, and many such subjects. He often argued though Religion is given to us at the time of birth, using that religion to love everyone is what God intended. There has been a lot of discussions about whether he practiced his religion, Islam.

When I started spending more time with him during his days as President of India I got to know he did follow the aspects of Islam. He made sure Friday prayers are scheduled properly and I also used to get invited if it was a holiday. The Holy Quran was his constant companion. He used to tell me that the more he read the Holy Quran more he had belief in the miracle of Allah. Everyday he used to read the translation and discuss with me one certain section from the Quran. He often mentioned that translation does not serve the purpose. To understand the Quran in total one should have learned Arabic at some point. But he equally spent time reading other Holy books to immerse himself deeper into spirituality.

It all started one day casually discussing Religion. It would be a cliche if I said he amazed me with his depth of knowledge. He asked me to read the book Muhammad by Karen Armstrong. We used to discuss at length the details Karen captured in the book. We matched it with the traditional knowledge passed on to us by elders. We then followed it with the History of Gods by Karen Armstrong to further discuss the topic. He had in his famous library many books and he used to lend me volumes of Hadith by Al Bhukari and others.

It was my first year with him in Delhi and the month of Ramadhan appeared in peak winter. He surprised me by saying let us fast this month and that he would make sure to manage his schedule. He was in his 70s at that time and he never showed any sign of tiredness after doing all his work while fasting. We used to eat something early in the morning and I would return from the office to break the fast with him. I was impatient and irritated and he was calm and collected during that period of time. But he never wanted anyone to know what he did with himself and religion.

The love for humanity would take him to join hands with Foundation for Understanding Religions and Enlightened Citizenship (FUREC). I have had a chance to experience a few of the works. I had one DVD produced by FUREC which had lectures on various religions given by leaders and it was amazing.

Grandpa experimented further with spirituality by writing books like 'Guiding Souls: Dialogues on the Purpose of Life' and 'Transcendence - My Spiritual Experiences'. I guess his real inspiration might have been fulfilled through another project.

One day I was busy getting into a Government building at Delhi for a meeting. I got a call from Grandpa. He straight away asked if I would be interested to go to the Haj pilgrimage with my 90-year-old maternal Grandpa. It was an enriching experience at a young age. I was only 23 years old at that time.

The Haj pilgrimage is one of the largest logistical operations in the world. In 2005, it involved more than 104 countries with 35 lakh people registering their presence. In the year 2005, India outranked Indonesia to register the most number of pilgrims. About 1,47,000 pilgrims performed, what is considered to be the final of the five important duties of the religion.

I had to be prepared both for the execution of the mission as well to perform the rituals properly. It took about four months by paying attention to every detail to prepare myself. Of course, we have modern-day communication like mobile phones, but the Haj pilgrimage has been happening for so many years even without it. People used to travel by ships for long time leaving their business and work.

The day came, with the blessings and prayers we set off to Jeddah. What followed was a remarkable human experience in the name of GOD. When we finally reached it was midnight in Mecca. It took about 2 hours to complete all the rituals including shaving off the head. It is always difficult to understand why people travel such a long distance and spend so much money to see a brick-walled cubicle. But I saw people crying at the first sight of Kaaba (called House of GOD). The Grand Mosque was a beautifully build mosque that can hold about 20 lakhs people.

We spent nearly about 40 days before it reached the climax in early January. In the meantime, we went for prayers every day 5 times and tried to live normally in the city. I used to go along with my grandfather in the early hours of the day to the mosque. We would take him in a wheelchair. Whenever we required some help, like lifting the wheelchair, there would be a person available providing a helping hand.

Day in and day out I saw orderliness in going in and coming out of the mosque. The crowd started building as the time moved on. For the

The day came, with the blessings and prayers we set off to Jeddah. What followed was a remarkable human experience in the name of GOD. When we finally reached it was midnight in Mecca.

prayer, on Friday we used to go as early as three hours before, only to sit under the hot sun with an umbrella. There was preparedness from the government to handle such a crowd. In the corner of a building, one could see paramedics with their stretcher and medical kit standing inconspicuously.

There were some interesting occasions also. In the morning at around 04:30 hrs local time we used to sit in the shivering cold waiting for the prayer to start. There was an African pilgrim who used to get up suddenly and start preaching. He was multi-lingual. He preached in many languages, starting from Arabic, English and ending with his mother tongue.

During the five days of Haj, the pilgrims have to stay in a tent at a place called Mina. The tents as it stands represents modern-day comfort homes. It was fully air-conditioned. It had well-built washrooms. It was made of fireproof tent material, cemented pavements, and beautifully lit exteriors. The tents of Arabian countries were a treat to watch.

On the first day, we spent time in the tents praying. It was told that it becomes really difficult to travel by vehicle than by walk. On the second day, we set off to a place called Arafat, which is about 14 kilometers in distance. By traveling in a vehicle we reached comfortably by forenoon. A few minutes before the sunset we took off to a place called Mustalifa about 7 kilometers away. By the time we reached the border of the place, it was 0200 hours in the night. Pilgrims walking were moving faster than us. At that place we had to spend the night in the open space. It is quite interesting to mention here is we were having only two-piece of unstitched clothes on us. As I slept in the ground only with a mat underneath me, my entire body felt frozen. One best part of the story is that I heard a Minister from a southern state who had come for the pilgrimage slept in the ground not even having a mat. Pilgrimages becomes a big leveler in front of the love of God.

Early in the morning, there was a huge queue for the washrooms. All the people otherwise would have fought in their homes for their turn were standing in absolute silence. In between, they were also allowing someone with deep trouble.

By the time we reached Mina back, it was 16:00 hours in the evening. In the night I went to perform the stone-throwing ritual and there were only a few people. This is the place prone to stampede due to many pilgrims turning up at the same time. On the third day, there was a stampede. I could not go exactly at that time, as I had to look after my grandfather. That saved my life. Probably there were some other divine plans for me. There were more than 50 pilgrims from our country who didn't see the light next day. The lot included Turks, Pakistanis, and Indians who are believed to be most perfect to follow the rituals even up to micro-level.

Finally, we reached Mecca again on the fifth day. However, there was one last ritual to be performed before coming back. It was the circum-ambulation of 7 times of Kaaba. I, with my clever intuition, went with my grandfather around 02:00 am in the night only to see at least 1 lakh pilgrims at that odd time.

Now at the end, even though it looks all simple, how 35 lakh pilgrims moved many times between Mecca, Mina, Arafat, Mustalifa is again a fact to ponder about. There are huge roads connecting these places. Still, pilgrims who walked reached in an hour while it took 8 to 12 hours to reach by a vehicle. It is also interesting to note that there was no problem with water anywhere in that desert. Food was always in abundance and in some places it was distributed free.

When we landed in Chennai, there was a sigh of relief and fulfillment to have performed one of the important rituals of the religion. But the mission taught more patience to me than in any given situation.

This was the biggest project I ever handled and ever was entrusted by Grandpa. He not only demanded organizational skills but also leadership from me to handle two seniors from my family. This was also his biggest inspirational event to immerse himself in spirituality. Grandpa mentions this in his book "Turning Points- A journey through challenges". The most interesting point is when he asked me to write that section for his book from his viewpoint. When the book came out he had taken my writing as is without any changes. I consider that as an honor to have written a page in one of the books of great author Dr. A.P.J. Abdul Kalam.

After this experience, I was pushing him to take the journey of Haj Pilgrimage himself. He told me that King of Saudi Arabia offered to host him as a State Guest to complete the Haj Pilgrimage. But Grandpa wanted to go as a normal pilgrim. But he had security cover all the time. These conflict of issues never allowed him to perform the Haj pilgrimage which remains a big disappointment for me. •

THE WRITER

Chapter 12

"Writing will test your mental strength",

- Dr. A.P.J. Abdul Kalam

Grandpa is known to be a good writer and orator. He inspired millions through his books and speeches. But like any genius, he had his own way of doing things. At the end of the 90s, we heard that Grandpa is writing an autobiography with Dr. Arun Tiwari. This was my first exposure to his way of writing books. He had sent a representative from the publisher to collect information and photographs. I automatically became the coordinator as I could speak little bit more English. We went through facts with the help of my maternal Grandpa A.P.J.M. Marakayar and spent time on collecting photographs. It was an excellent experience for me to learn about the making of a book. Little did I know that the book, 'Wings of Fire' would become a best seller and many of my friends would keep it in their prayer rooms.

I come from a family of avid readers. Never ever I had a shortage of books to read. Tamil is my mother tongue and respected in the family, a lot of books were available in Tamil literature and also in pop culture. But Wings of Fire changed my perception towards reading in English. I had a hard time understanding what Grandpa wanted to convey through that book. I could not comprehend why people appreciated it so much. All he wrote in that book was about technology. One day I had a chance to ask him. Grandpa explained that the book gave hope on two accounts. One a small village boy could be part of India's development in missiles and space program. Later I used to mention that a small village boy could become President of India. The second one being, how will and effort of the people like Dr. Vikram Sarabhai, Prof. Satish Dhawan and many more including Grandpa succeeded in making our nation self-reliant on space technology. I read the book again to experience further goose-bump moments.

His favorite place for relaxing was Library and he was always surrounded by a number of books. I always wondered how he could read all those books.

Fast-forwarding to 2003, Grandpa wanted to experiment with my writing skills. He started asking me to write pieces for his speeches as mentioned in the earlier chapters. I just did what he said without realizing his goal. He believed that reading helps in honing writing skills. He encouraged me to read books which he thought was useful. I will give a list of favorite books suggested by him at the end of this chapter. It will also have some interesting facts about reading those under his watch. This list changed and expanded over the years. I am giving this as a sample to show his deep interest in developing my reading habit.

He visualized the entire book in his mind first before writing it. Then he also visualized sections. He asked his staff to insert one particular section before another section as if referring to physical objects before him.

On one of those days, Grandpa was reviewing his upcoming book. He seemed to be not satisfied with the manuscript. His staff was already touching limits editing his book. To remind you these are the people churning out over 50 versions for one speech at his behest. They suggested him to give it to a fresh mind. Grandpa looked around and found me. He told me that I would get a copy of the manuscript and I had to edit and comment. He asked me how much time I needed. Before I answered I needed a month, he said ten days. I didn't know the subject and I never had experience of editing or commenting. I took that as a challenge.

I read the manuscript day and night. I was reading even while commuting to the office. My colleagues wondered about what I was reading. Finally, I handed over the manuscript. I corrected spelling mistakes and provided comments to improve the text and the flow. Grandpa accepted many of my suggestions. Of course, the manuscript further went into further changes before Grandpa agreed on the final script. That book "Indomitable Spirit" has a special name among the readers.

After Grandpa found out that I could work on manuscripts, he wanted to improve my writing by making me read a lot. He valued his books so much he was very reluctant to part with it even for a few days. His favorite place for relaxing was Library and he was always surrounded by a number of books. I always wondered how he could read all those books. He did master the art of reading books in his lifetime.

One funny thing about him was his possessiveness for books. He would passionately speak about a book that he has read.

Then he would ask me to read. I would quietly tell him that I would buy the book and read. But with enthusiasm, he used to offer his book for a few days. First time I didn't understand the implications of taking a book from him. Exactly after two days, he asked me to return the book. I had not even read ten pages in the book. I sheepishly returned to him without telling him that I had not completed the book. To my surprise, he started discussing the contents of the book. He eventually found out and mentioned how lazy I was towards reading the book. That day I understood the requirement and tried to live up to his expectation.

After having a good look at me, Grandpa encouraged me to write something on my own. This was particularly a big challenge. I have tried my hand in the past in Tamil writing but not in English. I was unable to decide for many days on what to write and medium of writing. Grandpa decided to step up the task

All he did was to make me comfortable, feel encouraged and teach me the art of writing in his own way. I am able to write coherently because Grandpa played a major role in making that happen.

and he asked me to write every week starting the following week. I was startled and kept on thinking. He asked me to write whatever comes to my mind.

I decided to write about my experiences and took up Blogs as the media. First time I wrote some long prose. He encouraged me after reading that. Then I got better by combining ideas I had from reading books, podcasts, people I met and based on the discussions with him. I called the blog with the name 'Mind Blowing'+. I thought once I reached the third week, he would not give attention to that project. I was wrong again.

As he would have very limited time, I used to take a printout and give him the week's blog post. He used to spend time reading it and wrote his comments in the side[3]. To my surprise, he used to bring that paper to the dinner table and discussed it with his friends on the ideas. I am not trying to paint a picture of how good my writing was. But to show how deep was the love of a Grandfather towards his little fellow. All he did was to make me comfortable, feel encouraged and teach me the art of writing in his own way. I am able to write coherently because Grandpa played a major role in making that happen.

[3] *If you would like to feel the love of a Grandfather, I have given few samples from my earlier blog for reference at the section Demo of love.*

One of the interesting incidents was when he handed me a paper with a poem on it. He told me to improve the poem that he had written in English. I had some experience of writing small poems in Tamil but this was my first ever attempt to improvise in English. He did accept a few of my changes and the final version had his signature style on it. Poems generally are considered to be linked to feelings. Poets consider them as a personal creation. This was the first time when I had to work on a poem. Grandpa, as usual, showed grace by accepting inputs. I went on to write few poems in Tamil and English. I never tried to publish then. I am happy because most of them were liked by Grandpa.

By the time Grandpa felt I had enough training in writing, he shifted his focus to get me prepared for the next project of my life.

BOOKS RECOMMENDED BY
Dr. A.P.J. Abdul Kalam

1. Light from many lamps, edited by Lillian Watson

I was struggling as a young man, living weekends in Rashtrapati Bhawan and spending other days to build a career. Grandpa somehow sensed my problem and recommended this book. I found solace in reading sections like courage and peace of mind.

2. Man the Unknown, Alexis Carrell

I borrowed this book one fine day from Grandpa. He told me I had 2 days to read the book and have to summarize it to him in the end. I managed to read it but explained to him that I needed time to reflect on the book to summarize to him.

3 Thirukural, Thiruvalluvar

Grandpa liked Thirukkural very much. He often referred couplets during casual discussions also. He also used to give explain the couplet in a different way which I disagreed with sometimes. This led to a lot of arguments between us. Whenever there was a chance he mentioned Thirukkural in his speeches.

4. Empires of Mind, Denis Waitley

Grandpa disliked giving direct career advice to me. But he also wanted to convey his ideas on career and a glimpse of the future. This book certainly opened my mind to how to work and live in a fast-paced world.

5. A History Of God, Karen Armstrong

Grandpa wanted to give a mild lesson on theology to me. This book was his way of introducing the subject. We used to discuss a lot later on theology, spirituality and human life.

6. Physics of the Future: The Inventions that will Transform our Lives, Michio Kaku

I worked on promoting new technologies to Industry in my career. Grandpa wanted to further enhance my understanding of technology trends. This book was a perfect match to read and discuss the technological developments of the future. •

THE FAMILY MAN

"If a country is to be corruption free and become a nation of beautiful minds, I strongly feel there are three key societal members who can make a difference. They are the father, the mother and the teacher."

- Dr. A. P. J. Abdul Kalam

Grandpa has always been a thorough family man. That was the reason he could care for his colleagues' and friends' families. A very interesting incident below summaries how he cared for the family.

During one of those my Delhi years I was traveling on a train to Chennai and then on to reach Rameswaram. The plan was to reach home to celebrate Eid. The train got delayed for 10 hours and got rerouted. This was due to incessant rain and flooding on the normal route. The alternate route had no stopping stations. Due to this all the water in the coaches ran out. There was no food available. I was also fasting during the journey. Grandpa had sent along with me a basket of fruits. My friend who was traveling along with me shared the fruits with fellow passengers.

Grandpa was in touch all through the journey. He started getting worried about my fasting despite the problems. I had saved one pouch of water to break the fast because the train was running non-stop. Due to thirst one of my fellow passengers started collapsing. They started asking for water as he was dehydrated. The only choice was to give up my pouch of water. The passenger was in a very high position in an educational institution. He woke up and started worrying for me. But he said God would be with us.

Grandpa was talking to me now and then and I told him that I have no water now. He took a long breath and asked me whether the fellow passenger was doing fine. He then told me that God would help me find whatever I wanted. His words came true and we found food and water in the evening. I had saved two fruits for breaking the fast. With the strength of friends around and Grandpa's words, I survived the journey. I also continued my Ramzan fasting the next day.

The next day my friend and I were sitting on a bus in Chennai to travel to Madurai. Grandpa called in the morning and checked how long I would take to reach home. He realized I would not be able to reach home for Eid celebrations. We were about an hour into the bus when we heard some commotion and bus driver was trying to stop the bus on the side of the road. My friend told me that my name was being called out of a car. The bus stopped and people were looking for me on the bus. Though I got afraid, I identified myself. The person told me that the President of India, Dr. Abdul Kalam has asked them to take me home fast. Grandpa with all his work was able

Grandpa made a promise to attend my wedding as he has not attended a family wedding for almost 19 years. We fixed the date in consultation with him.

to make travel arrangements for me to reach home to celebrate Eid.

Grandpa later turned his attention to getting me married. He kept following up and when I finally told him we found a match, he said, "I want to attend your wedding".

Grandpa made a promise to attend my wedding as he has not attended a family wedding for almost 19 years. We fixed the date in consultation with him. The town of Ramanathapuram has not seen such a wedding for a long time. Not because of anything else, but for the presence of the great son of the soil Dr. Abdul Kalam himself. People from all walks of life for the love of him thronged to the wedding venue just to get a glimpse of him. My wife and I were seeing him going around the venue. People were following him, like a powerful magnet that attracts iron particles.

Grandpa kept reminding people to bless the couple as this was the reason he had come. He refused to sit on the stage. He asked my maternal Grandpa to do the signatures in the wedding register while everyone wanted him to sign. He also brought with him well thought out gifts. The gifts might look strange for many. But he brought those gifts which he thought had value and uniqueness. A watch presented to him by Sri Satya Sai Baba, a bottle of honey from North East India and the signed copy of his book "Indomitable Spirit". He said I needed the indomitable spirit to cross the "Samsara Saaharam" (translates as an ocean of married life). I was pleased as this was the book I had provided my help earlier. He also put a ring on my wife's finger. He told me later, "I have given a ring to my granddaughter". This showed he already accepted my wife into his family.

My work took me to different locations within the city and to different cities where I lived. Grandpa made it a point to visit each of those locations. He came and celebrated the birth of my children and amused at their first steps. Though very strict in diet, he relished on dishes prepared by my wife to make her happy.

Life has its ups and downs. A relationship faces challenges during life many a time. Either we grow up or some external stimuli disturbs the peace. I faced such a situation in my life. I realized that working on a relationship is important rather than taking it for granted.

Grandpa chose someone from the family for an important

project. He thought that person was the right choice. Because family politics pushed on a candidate unsuitable for his requirement. The project failed. Out of jealousy, the candidate damaged my reputation with Grandpa by spinning stories. The candidate got a lot of help from different family members. They were too jealous of my closeness to Grandpa. So they helped him to get an opportunity to separate me from Grandpa.

Till that time I was considering my relationship with Grandpa was only about love. But others were thinking on the lines of getting favors, money, fame, position, and power. I also committed my share of mistakes due to my situation and gullibility.

One day Grandpa suddenly stopped talking to me. As mentioned earlier I lost connection with someone who understood me completely. I was left in unimaginable sorrow of my life and did not know the way to correct it.   •

ANGEL OF HOPE Chapter 14

"When a problem arises, become the captain of the problem and defeat it!"

- Dr. A.P.J. Abdul Kalam

Grandpa and I fell out of touch for sometime. It was due to the misunderstandings between us and also due to our work. We used to have a habit of sharing our important travel plans. This was to make sure that we do not call each other during travel. I was planning on a ten-day official trip to Australia. But this time I did not tell him.

All went well on the trip except suddenly I developed a high fever one day. Fever worsened and I had difficulty in breathing. It was the last day of the trip and I decided to come back as I had medicines given by the doctor whom I had seen in Adelaide. But when I landed in Singapore, the fever was burning and I had difficulty in walking. I somehow reached the emergency medical center in Singapore Airport. The doctor checked my saturation (Oxygen in my blood) and made me rest in the bed. He immediately started antibiotics through IV drips and somehow reduced my fever. He then told me very calmly that I have to be admitted to the hospital as my lungs were infected. He also asked me to cancel my remaining part of the trip to Chennai. I adamantly refused and took the flight to Chennai.

The next day along with my wife I went to see the doctor and ended up in Apollo hospitals. Then all went blank. The rest of the things could be best said in the words of my Grandpa. By the grace of GOD as I lived to tell this story, Grandpa went to Apollo for a speech and used it as thanksgiving opportunity.

Excerpt from the Speech by Grandpa - Address and interaction with Doctors and Staff of Apollo Hospital, Chennai, Jan 6, 2014

When I am with you, I would like to talk on the topic "The Great Hospital:".

Let me start by sharing my recent experience with Apollo Hospital.

In early October this year one my grandsons Gulaam got admitted to Apollo hospitals Chennai complaining high fever and breathing difficulties. The fever continued for a few days and we were worried. At one point of time the fever reached at a very high level. I rushed to the hospital to my grandson's room at the Critical Care Unit around 2:00 am. There was hardly any space as the room was full of doctors, nurses and other medical assistants. They were putting ice cubes and three fans were blowing cold air to bring the fever under control. That was the situation my grandson went through at various stages including forced sleep with sedation, breathing with ventilator support, almost for a month.

As you are aware about the diagnosis, treatment and after care, all are related to hospitalization. Apollo Hospitals came out as a champion in all the areas related to the incident I mentioned about my grandson. I discussed the situation with your chairman Dr. Prathap Reddy. He immediately formed a multi-disciplinary team across India and also consulted experts from abroad. This team monitored the situation and discussed every day on the treatment progress and the way forward. The hospital provided the best of the technology available in the treatment.

When I landed in Singapore, the fever was burning and I had difficulty in walking. I somehow reached the emergency medical center in Singapore Airport.

This is all expected from an institution of repute like Apollo. I would like to talk about the culture and the DNA which has been built by the Chairman and strictly followed by the team of doctors and staff.

During the initial stages when the fever was high, a critical care doctor was always present in the room. The doctors lead by Dr. Narashiman was on call at all the times and spent sleepless nights to monitor the situation. The nurses at the critical care unit provided hope by pointing out all positive responses. They worked on him and took personal care, keeping him groomed and provided tips on facing the doctors so that he would get positive review. One of the nurses asked him to wave at the doctors every time they come to visit him. This resulted in rare mention by the doctors in the file as 'patient is cheerful' instead of patient is responsive. The nurses also shared with him stories about their pleasant lives to get him go sleep. They played crosswords, helped holding iPads and newspapers. When Gulaam was very weak even to get up, they provided immense hope and let him walk with six people surrounding him. The physiotherapists gave him tough movements with ease and gave lot of moral support.

When my grandson got out of the hospital, he said one thing, that mattered a lot apart from the treatment was the personal care given to him by the Apollo hospitals. The care went beyond doctors, nurses, paramedics to even the housekeeping staff who told my grandson that they prayed to God for his recovery. Of course not to forget the Chairman Dr. Prathap Reddy who visited my grandson personally and extracted a promise that he would run before him to show that the treatment got him better. Ghulaam grandpa is about 97 years old. He visited him on the critical day and prayed and prayed for his well being. My 97 years old brother said in the Apollo hospital, "My grandson is in Allah's custody". He had full faith on the treatment given by Apollo. This was proved by the Apollo team and Gulaam got cured fully from his ailment and walked out of their hospital after completely cured.

This culture is the unique quality of Apollo hospitals where every single member of this family works hard to get the patient better. I would say all of you are "Angels of Hope" and

It would be a half story without talking about my wife in this chapter. She stood strong despite all odds were against. She handled Grandpa's demands which brought her close to him.

wish you all the best to lift many other suffering souls out of misery. Thank you.

❧❧❧❧❧❧❧❧❧❧❧

Grandpa was my Angel of Hope during that difficult time. Grandpa visited me as soon as I woke up. I have written briefly about this in the Prologue of this book. But what is missing from the prologue as well as Grandpa's speech is the emotions attached to this whole episode. The rest of the chapter is described from what I heard from my wife, my family, Grandpa and my colleagues.

As soon as my condition became worse, my wife called my office, Confederation of Indian Industry. Luckily, Mr. Mahesh Natarajan, my reporting manager was the Regional Director. He was responsible for the entire southern region in CII. He is also a good friend. CII is known to be a humane organization taking care of the employees at difficult times. Quickly a team of colleagues was requested to help my family at the hospital.[4] It would be an injustice to just mention few names of my

[4] *My team members from TNTDPC, Chennai deserve a special mention here. They forgot their families to look after me during that time. They spend time in hospital in shifts and slept in most unaccommodating places. They also kept the work running so that there was no effect on my absence. This was compassion shown at the highest levels.*

colleagues. These colleagues are highly qualified, have long experience. But they all came together to help me come out of the hospital. CII also footed the bill for my long hospitalization. CII paid salary for that period without batting an eyelid. My wife also got various forms of support throughout my stay in hospital. A special thanks goes to former Director General Mr. Tarun Das, present Director General Mr. Chandrajit Banerjee and my manager, Mr. Anjan Das with whom I served the longest for providing such a wonderful support.

When my condition became serious, my wife informed Grandpa. Grandpa without hesitation told her that he would come the next day. He made a special trip to see me the next day. He then made my wife, the center of all information flow. Grandpa took over the major responsibility of coordinating with the hospital at the highest level. But later he told me slowly emotions took over and he started feeling sorry for me. After a few days, my condition worsened further and my wife called Grandpa around 1:00 am. Doctors had very slim hope that I would survive that night. Luckily Grandpa was staying in Raj Bhawan Chennai on that day.

Grandpa without thinking started in the car to the hospital. He reached and started working with the doctors. They decided to turn my sleeping position to make me breathe better. By 3:00 am I got better and Grandpa was satisfied to return to Raj Bhawan. He returned the next morning. My maternal Grandpa from Rameswaram also visited at that time. Both of them prayed their hearts out. I guess God was compelled to accept their prayers because of their advanced age and due to the show of love.

The important fact is that at 1:00 am on that night there were no proper arrangements available for him to travel. He requested the Governor for a car and came with two security personnel. Most part of his life Grandpa was provided with Z plus security by the Government. But love for his grandson made Grandpa forget everything to visit the hospital at that time. I later learned that Grandpa kept on asking many doctors about the solution to my situation. He kept repeating to others it was very unfortunate. I could never imagine him in such a mental state at any point in time.

All his life he dedicated his mind and body to the development of the country. But this time love for me weakened him. During this period prayer meetings were organized at the offices of CII. A few of my colleagues shed tears for me. I can never be thankful enough in my lifetime to them.

When I woke up Grandpa came to see me in the Critical care unit (CCU). He with his trademark smile told me that he was counting days when I could reach home. After I reached home he again visited me. This time with gifts for my children to make them happy. While going back he told me to give him a small write up to include in his speech at Apollo hospitals. I was very weak and was unable to move my fingers. But he insisted I send him. I typed in the IPad and completed a draft. He liked the title Angles of hope and told me that he would retain it. But he in his own way changed it to suit his style. I watched the live streaming of the program from home. When Grandpa completed this particular section, Dr. Pratap Reddy, Founder of Apollo Hospitals became emotional. He got up from his seat, went up to Grandpa and held his hand. Dr. Pratap Reddy was himself involved in my case and later called me "Miracle Man of Apollo".

It would be a half story without talking about my wife in this chapter. She stood strong despite all odds were against. She handled Grandpa's demands which brought her close to him. He kept calling her "Jabeen Amma" with love because she took care of his grandson. She was strong enough to bring me out of death, put me back on my legs and still tolerate my eccentricities. Grandpa told me that she gave half her life and energy to save me.

When I was barely walking, Grandpa pushed me to attend the office. With his comforting words, I drove myself to the office and walked-in one day, just like that. Grandpa was pleased and asked me to come to his Delhi house with family. A deadly virus and God's grace united me with Grandpa disintegrating all differences.   •

THE GREAT GRANDFATHER

"One of the very important characteristics of a student is to question. Let the students ask questions."

- Dr. A. P. J. Abdul Kalam

Grandpa played all the roles mentioned till now with ease. Life wanted him to play one more role as Great Grandfather to my children. He did that with ease as if Sachin Tendulkar scoring a fluent century.

Grandpa on the last leg of the innings as the President of India was offered a big residence. But he could not decide on those big residences. Finally, Grandpa agreed to a compact residence at 10, Rajaji Marg, New Delhi. The residence became the center of our activities later on. In 2016 I had a chance to speak at the birthday celebrations of Grandpa at Rashtrapati Bhawan. Honorable President of India Shri Ramnath Kovind presided over the function. I mentioned in my speech that I loved visiting Rashtrapati Bhawan because Grandpa was residing there. Honorable President of India appreciated the meaning behind those words with a smile.

> My dear great Grandson
>
> In the few years
> you will read
> "The Luminous sparks"
>
> It is a beautiful book
> of poems, paintings
> and beautiful Thoughts
> all around us.
>
> May the Almighty bless
> you, on the Birth Day.
>
> A.P.J. Abdul Kalam
> 21/10/09

Grandpa's presence made the place special. Thus for the next eight years, Rajaji Marg residence became a special place to go to. The grass was greener, the birds chirped little more, the wind blew more softly, monkeys jumped a bit more, roses smiled a lot and love filled the rest of the space. Grandpa also showed more of his multi-faceted nature here to us.

Grandpa loved playing with my children. Of course, his love for students and children is well known. He often said he gets good attention from children than the grown-up people. He listened to their interest and played games according to their needs. Cricket was one of those games. He actively played with them which was a surprise to me. These were also the years that saw the rise of Indian cricket. I witnessed the Indian cricket team's triumph in two big championships.

It was the final match of the Inaugural T20 Championship held in South Africa. I was traveling with a delegation on Nanotechnology from the United Kingdom across the country. When the delegation reached Kolkata it was raining very heavily. Some areas were flooded. Luckily we got into the van and quickly got away from a flooded area. Still we had to go to the dinner reception hosted by British Deputy High Commissioner at his residence. I was talking to Grandpa in between as he was worried for two reasons. It was raining heavily and also I was keeping the Ramzan fasts during the travel. We also discussed the finals coming up and I told him that it would be difficult for me to enjoy the match.

The delegation members both from India and the United Kingdom while having dinner was restless. They were indeed cricket lovers and wanted to know about the finals. When the formalities were over the host invited us to watch the cricket match with him on TV. This

I had a chance to speak at the birthday celebrations of Grandpa at Rashtrapati Bhawan. Honorable President of India Shri Ramnath Kovind presided over the function.

was one time when I saw Britishers cheering for India. Grandpa after listening to all this story invited me to residence when such an event happens.

Destiny has its way of making the words of wise true. I landed up in Delhi for the final match of the 2011 Cricket World Cup. Grandpa does not watch the television. But he asks his staff or me about the course of the game. He was thrilled that the Indian team reached the finals. As his residence always resembles a holy place there was only one television at the visitor's room. Grandpa was making more rounds than usual to know about the game. When India finally won the cup he was very happy and pleased. I realized he wanted to see India triumph in each and every field.

Grandpa always found unique things at the places where he stayed. At Rajaji Marg, it was Jamun (Indian Blackberry/ Naavar Pazham) and Roses. He nurtured Rose plants at his residence. Different varieties blossomed there; some with fragrance some with color. He would spend a good amount of time talking to the gardener to make him understand his care towards the plants. Every morning he would ask his great-grand-kids to go and count the Roses. He would then walk with them to identify the Roses with fragrance. The next question was to identify the colors. He made learning fun for the kids. Jamun was seasonal and he waited for the season. He made sure good ones are picked up and he tried his best to make the kids eat them. Jamun became a special fruit as it was offered by Grandpa to us.

Grandpa was worried about the children not eating properly. He would spend close to an hour making my younger son eat by telling him stories. He would then take them to some other place and start teaching them. On one of those days when my three-year-old son was not listening to him, he asked him how many slaps he could give. My son's answer was Zero. Encouraged by the answer Grandpa asked him how many chocolates he wanted. When he got the answer 'infinity', he told me that my son was better prepared to face this world. He further encouraged them to ask him difficult questions. So the children asked him why it took so long to reach the moon. Grandpa was excited. He asked for a paper, started making all kinds of drawings and explained with enthusiasm. In short few minutes, he taught them about perigee, apogee, earth's rotation, revolution, geosynchronous orbit, use of earth's gravity to slingshot satellite launch vehicles, distance to moon and how India would plan to do that. Grandpa did watch the success of Chandrayaan-1 and Mangalyaan -1. He made sure his great-grand-kids knew about ISRO's feat. It was also a proud moment when I saw Grandpa directing his great-grand kids to launch paper rockets at a target.

On one of those days, Grandpa was watching the kids play. Suddenly my younger son was lost. The property is well protected by the Delhi Police and Central Industrial Security Force (CISF). So there was no doubt about safety. First, we started searching normally. But after half an hour we could not find him. He asked his staff to start searching. They also could not find him. Grandpa was worried and by that time we had

gone around the house many times. Finally he decided to call the Delhi police team stationed at the house. But luckily one of his staff members had experience in handling mischievous children. He went again to the office room. He started looking below the tables. My son was found hiding below a table and he was all smiling to have made fool of us. Grandpa told me that I had dangerous fellows at home (on a lighter note) and to be careful dealing with them. I could feel the love from Grandpa and saw how he was willing to go any extent to find the child in a short time.

In March 2015, Grandpa again called me with the family to stay with him for ten days. He kept himself free to play with his great-grand sons. But I could see some change in him. He was like someone who reached a point of contentedness. He was at peace and his joy was spilling all over the place. We sat down together as we were watching the children play on the lawns. He said that the children have grown up and they are not babies anymore. He then told me to take good care of them. It sounded very disturbing to me. So I asked him, "Would you send my children to college?". He smiled knowing that it was years away. He also understood I was playing with words to get him to commit to living longer. He took a deep breath and said, "You are asking too much from this life buddy".

Grandpa's last book "Transcendence -My special experiences with Pramukh Swamiji" was of a different kind. Though he gave a copy to me I could not read it. Later, Prof. Arun Tiwari, the co-author quoted this line from page number 50 of this book.

"He is the ultimate stage of spiritual ascent in my life, which started with my father, was sustained by Dr. Brahma Prakash and Prof. Sathish Dhawan; now, finally Pramukh Swamiji has put me in a God-synchronous orbit. No maneuvers are required any more, as I am placed in my final position in eternity." •

THE MARGADARSI Chapter 16

"BHARAT has lost a Ratna, but the light from this jewel will guide us towards APJ Abdul Kalam's dream-destination: India as a knowledge superpower, in the first rank of nations."

- The Prime Minister of India, Shri Narendra Modi

Why do so many people love Dr. A.P.J. Abdul Kalam? Why did more than one lakh people turn up at his funeral at Rameswaram when security was so tight? Why did people cry inconsolably whom they have never met? What made a seventy-five-year-old person to travel in the bus a long distance to come and pay respect? Is it because he spent his entire life dedicated to this nation and the people? Is it because he was a role model of hope and success? Is being alive necessary to teach someone? Can the death of someone teach millions of people values? There are no answers I could find. But Grandpa did go away by taking a piece of people's heart with him and leaving his piece with them.

A day is enough to turn the history of nations. A day is enough to change anyone's life forever. There are days that become an inflection point in life. A before and after the stage is created in life with a void so big which makes it impossible to cross over between the stages. July 27, 2015, was one such fateful day in my life. Even when I was struggling with my life in a hospital bed I could wake up to Grandpa's smiling face. But on 27th July 2015 I woke into a dream never to come back to normal life.

In my entire life being together with Grandpa I was used to getting hoax messages about his death. At one point in time, there was a message where he was kept in a hospital for more than 15 days. We were laughing reading that message together. Whenever I get such message I used to verify with his office to make sure false message is not spread. On 27th July 2015, I was not watching television. Around 7:30 pm, I got a call from my friend that news channels are showing that Dr. Abdul Kalam has passed away. I could not believe it. I also not wanted to believe it. I thought this was another hoax call. But when I called his office, they were also fighting to believe that news.

Like a dream, I got myself together to the airport the next day early morning to catch a flight from Bangalore to New Delhi. I along with my cousin went to New Delhi to take care of matters there. We reached the Rajaji Marg residence and started waiting for the mortal remains to arrive. Again the organization I worked in, Confederation of Indian Industry (CII), an organization with a heart took care of my needs during that difficult time. Later in the day my wife and children also joined me at New Delhi and children could not believe their 'Appa' was no more.

On the morning of 28th July, Grandpa reached Palam airport. Among the dignitaries were President of India Shri Pranab Mukherjee, Prime Minister Shri Narendra Modi and many more. There was also Marshal of Indian Air Force Arjan Singh in the wheelchair. A war hero of the 1965 war with Pakistan. He paid one of the unforgettable tributes to Grandpa. He stood up from his wheelchair, fully dressed in uniform, walked with the help of a stick to lay a wreath and saluted majestically.

When the coffin reached Rajaji Marge residence, I lost all my courage to look at

When the coffin reached Rajaji Marge residence, I lost all my courage to look at Grandpa. I even now do not have the courage to look at his last speech at IIM Shillong, nor can I hear the audio.

Grandpa. I even now do not have the courage to look at his last speech at IIM Shillong, nor can I hear the audio. Moments passed when I had to perform my duty of talking to the visitors. The whole parliament was there including Sachin Tendulkar whom I always wanted to meet. All those moments passed as if it was a dream.

When the Prime Minister Shri Narendra Modi arrived, I was still in tears. He rested his hand on my shoulder and comforted me. He also mentioned that he never knew about the family of

Dr. Abdul Kalam. That summarized the way Grandpa kept his public life and family life separate. I cried most at that moment.

Time rolled on and visitors were continually pouring in even towards midnight. We requested a few minutes to offer a prayer for the night. In the early hours of the next day, we prepared ourselves to start on a long journey to carry Grandpa to Rameswaram.

As we walked out the tri-forces; Army, Navy and Air Force, paid tribute. The tri-force officers carried the coffin. Here and there I was asked by media questions about how I felt and what we were planning to do to continue his legacy. I do not remember those answers. We entered Palam airport and a military transport aircraft was waiting for us to take to Madurai. This was the first time I had to travel in an army aircraft. Grandpa could give me that experience even after he decided to have a long sleep. The only missing thing was he did not call me to work with him on that long flight.

Grandpa could give me that experience even after he decided to have a long sleep. The only missing thing was he did not call me to work with him on that long flight.

We landed in Madurai and Grandpa received full State honors with all armed forces present. The fellow soldiers transferred Grandpa to a helicopter. We also got ourselves into the helicopter. My younger son kept asking what happened to Appa. He did not want to accept reality. It was again an ordeal journey to the helipad near Rameswaram. We heard on the way that State Government of Tamil Nadu has given a resting place at Peikarumbu for Grandpa.

We landed at Rameswaram in the evening. I went through motions on that day. Grandpa's mortal remains were kept for the public to pay respect. Then we proceeded to home for family rituals. My maternal Grandpa was inconsolable. I saw him in tears for the first time in my life. Seeing a hundred-year-old crying was heart-melting. The whole night people from many walks of life, students, and relatives paid tribute.

The next day morning, we started towards the burial ground. All the set up was taken care of by the State Government. Including Prime Minister of India, all dignitaries were present. I coordinated between tri-forces, like always, only this time finally to lay Grandpa to rest. After everyone paid respect, tri-force soldiers handed over the National flag to my Grandpa. My maternal Grandpa insisted that the relatives should lay

Grandpa to rest. The soldiers handed over Grandpa's body to us. He carried me in his heart all his life. He felt light as I was carrying for him for the first time. We slowly lowered him into his resting place. My legs buckled because of the emotional weight.

Thousands of people flooded the place to pay respects once the dignitaries left. They were from all walks of society. There were youngsters, children, women, and senior citizens. I saw one formally dressed man in his seventies struggling through the crowd. We later found that he was a retired Principal of a school and came all by himself to pay respect. There were many such stories that were captured by the media.

A memorial was later built by the Defense Research Development Organisation (DRDO), Grandpa's alma mater. Till today lakhs and lakhs of people visit the place to gain a piece of light from him.

PM Modi paid tribute to Grandpa by calling him, his marg darshak who epitomized values of self-restraint, sacrifice & compassion.

On contemplating the questions on what was Dr. A.P.J. Abdul Kalam to the people, I could come to only one conclusion. He is their guide, the Margadarsi. taking them towards the dream of developed India. He is the hope of millions of students who dreamed to become like him.

Dr. A.P.J. Abdul Kalam, my Grandpa is the light of the Ignited Minds. •

DEMO OF LOVE

I have given few samples of my writing in this section.

This is to showcase the love of my Grandpa in appreciating my work to further develop me.

MIND BLOWING

(A special blog written for Grandpa)

Few Select Posts

INNER BEAUTY

Saturday, April 22, 2006

I recently had to come across a word in Hindi, which refers to inner glow or radiance. Radiance always seems to be synonymous with inside out action. Sun radiates light and energy. But how there can be the inner glow from a human being. We might have read so many books and articles referring to inner beauty from simple to most complicated ways for human understanding. There are spiritual gurus who talk day in and day out about radiance and the human mind.

The argument here is how does that translate to a normal human being. He/she starts the day around 6:00 am in the morning and reach home again around 7:00-8:00 pm in the night, leaving little time to talk to the family. Is this not a good period for us to think about inner beauty. Maybe that is why spirituality has been a topic for elder people. Otherwise younger people are only attracted to wipe away their temporary worries so that the system does not break down.

I am trying to explore the inner beauty in my own context and experience. To start with we suddenly like someone for no reason and hate someone else on the other hand. To put it simply, I read a quote saying, "Everyone you see in your life is the reflection of yourself". Hence we can take that the people we like are the reflection of our good things. For example we may be good at dressing, talking and when we see someone doing that in a similar way, we may tend to like them. It works same way out with the hating principle. I may hate someone biting his/her nail. This is the habit I am trying to get rid for so many years.

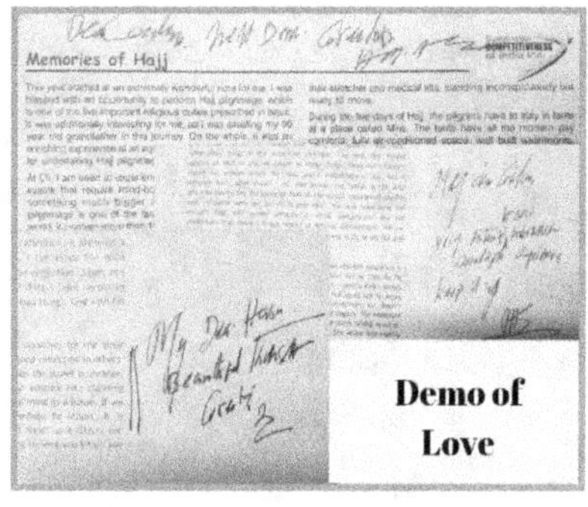

Demo of Love

Having said that, out of jealousy we may hate people even if they are our good reflections. It gives a sense of insecurity and competition for our ego.

Interestingly some of us would love to see our bad reflections in others. For example an angry person might find solace with another angry person, which gives a sense of satisfaction that he/she is not alone. All along I have experienced in my life all the above combinations.

One improvement in me is that I started seeing all the combinations in other people rather than stamping them for one reflection. It presents a good opportunity to learn by looking at others. I can enjoy the good reflections and try to change myself from a bad reflection. Again one has to consider here that good or bad reflection differs from person to person. There is no standard glossary of good and bad things. God with his usual supremacy left it to humans to decide.

Coming back to the point, we have to look into ourselves for inner beauty. My way of doing it would be to start seeing good reflection in others. This is same as keeping your house clean even when the street is unclean. Slowly everyone will clean their houses and also venture into cleaning their streets. This can be applied similar to human mind as a house. If we start developing a good mind, it will start radiate to others. It is important to help others to spiritually clean their minds as it affects you also. It requires great deal of patience and learning to keep you intact and help others.

Leaving good minds to subject matter of discretion we can look for socially accepted norms. It is like avoiding corruption on every possible occasion, helping someone to get a job (may not be poor), motivating your colleague during bad times, being present with someone when they lose their near ones and so on. These are very small improvements, which catches with others. At least for the sake of societal pressures someone will start practicing.

It will harness the beauty of the mind and also give a sense of satisfaction of having done something useful. The beauty would reflect in the face and give a glow to the body. It will attract more minds, which are struggling to sense their beauty. It will result in a win-win situation for the person as well as the people around.

I wish you for welcoming inner beauty into your mind homes. •

COLD WATER

Sunday, May 21, 2006

Water is a burning issue in terms of a sustainable environment and food security for all nations. The Arabian countries are spending a lot of oil-rich money for desalination of seawater. We had started taking water availability for granted long time back. Water conservation never had an impact on place like Chennai, where the problem is more pronounced. When the state government made rainwater harvesting compulsory, the people responded without any enthusiasm. The same people vote down the government (almost) every five years considering water availability as one of the issues.

Facts about water may not be interesting to need, even though about two-thirds of the human body is made of water. Toilet flushing is considered to be the single largest use of water at homes followed by bathing and washing. A low-flush toilet would use about 6 liters of water per flush. Moving on to human consumption front, only 1% of the water is only suitable. About 97% of water is saltwater. This leaves very little scope for thinking of drinking water for future.

We have started realizing that drinking water costs more than aerated drinks. Our friends might agree in countries like USA, more often you would see a person with a bottle of aerated drink than bottle of water in the hand. But on the other side, it has helped small business units for water recycling, packaging and distribution to thrive in far-reaching places. This also promoted spreading of unsafe drinking water in the market. Innovative people collect water bottles from trains, refill and sell it to the same people.

Hearing about cold water brings a shy of relief during hot summer days. My recent years in New Delhi have helped to understand the need for cold water. On Sundays, it used to be scorching hot under the roof. We try to live with minimum available resources for ease of moving around. The only consolation would be air cooler, which blows out hot air. The water from the tank would be hot enough to keep us warm.

During lunchtimes, we used to go to a restaurant particularly. The reason for our visit even though it is little costlier than the rest was the cold water. The restaurant used to serve cold water for the customers. Of course, we could have bought a bottle of chilled water or purchased a refrigerator. But the enjoyment we had while drinking the water as if it was given free is much more compared to the above. By the time we finish our lunch, the water intake used to be more than the food. To tackle this problem, we purchased a mud pot. One of my friends fills it in the morning sincerely. In the evening he will see an empty pot, as it would have leaked all over the house. Sometimes during transit of the pot, they had made openings at both sides (by breaking the bottom of the pot).

With these small incidents what comes to the mind is anything in abundance doesn't catch the much-needed attention of the people. On the other hand, fulfilling small requirements really brings happiness in life than through a larger need. One has to strike a balance between the requirement and the usage of anything in life, which would help the world prosper in a more definitive way. More responsible usage of world resources would bring prosperity in a much shorter time than visualized. •

PROFESSIONS !

Friday, August 18, 2006

We celebrated our 60th Independence Day recently. Only on this day, we start thinking, what we have done for this country. This is most of the time influenced by movies like "Rang De Basanti" and other nationalistic songs on the television channels. The next day routine catches up with us and we forget all these things. Television channels search for another movie for next year's Independence Day. But if someone asks, what should I do, the answer was found in the oath administered by the President of India to the school children. It roughly says, whatever work you do, do at your best. This is to wipe away the thought that only armed services or social development are the professions that renders direct impact on national development. We are going to see three professions from three different sects of society and understand how they are really important.

It was the time when I was working with a National research laboratory in Bangalore. To spend leisure, I used to listen to the radio. At that time the FM revolution had started. In one particular channel, I liked a Radio Jockey (RJ) for the mere fluency and presence of mind. She would talk for hours and hours in English, which fascinated me. Furthermore, she doesn't belong to that region and hosts the shows only in English. The important aspect I noticed is that before playing a song she starts talking about it. She continues when the background music plays. She would stop exactly before the first word of the song is played. She would do it again and again without missing the timing. After 3 years when I heard the channel again, she had graduated to host different shows. The RJs now hail from the local place and speak mix of Kannada and English effortlessly.

The second profession is a very interesting one. I stand everyday waiting for my official vehicle at a bus stop. I see an entrepreneur who sells large ice bars. He waits for the truck carrying the ice bars. He would then transport his requirement to the pavement. He would then carry it in a scooter to distribute it to shops. There is a tingle of enthusiasm in his eyes, even if he does the same thing. There is a sense of responsibility when he puts off his cigarette when he reaches for his son. I see a great feeling of achievement when he finishes his work and takes his son in the same scooter for dropping him in the school.

I was having dinner one day in a small restaurant. A young

foreigner sat in the table next to me. I was amazed when I heard him speak. He started ordering in Tamil. My friend who was sitting near to him could not resist. He started talking to him. I learned from my friend that the young man was from USA. He is a volunteer in one of the NGOs working for helping HIV patients. He had spent nearly about 5 years in Madurai and learned to speak local dialect fluently. Since he had to work with the residents of the local region, he had to learn the language. He has got accustomed to food and culture. He came back after some time to New Delhi and he searched for this south Indian restaurant. I see him often nowadays and I am very sure he will speak Hindi fluently in future.

All three examples bring out only one single message. The RJ giving information about heritage of Bangalore or the entrepreneur supplying ice bars on time or the young man helping the patients, they all do their work with enthusiasm, application, determination, and commitment. Only social development cannot transform the nation unless there is economic development. Economic development can only fuel social development to uplift the rest of society. Economic development can come only through the great work of you and me. Hence if whatever work we do, if we do the best, we are contributing to the development of the Nation.

We celebrated our 60th Independence Day recently. Only on this day, we start thinking, what we have done for this country. This is most of the time influenced by movies like "Rang De Basanti" and other nationalistic songs on the television channels. The next day routine catches up with us and we forget all these things. Television channels search for another movie for next year's Independence Day. But if someone asks, what should I do, the answer was found in the oath administered by the President of India to the school children. It roughly says, whatever work you do, do at your best. This is to wipe away the thought that only armed services or social development are the professions that renders direct impact on national development. We are going to see three professions from three different sects of society and understand how they are really important.

It was the time when I was working with a National research laboratory in Bangalore. To spend leisure, I used to listen to the radio. At that time the FM revolution had started. In one particular channel, I liked a Radio Jockey (RJ) for the mere fluency and presence of mind. She would talk for hours and hours in English, which fascinated me. Furthermore, she doesn't belong to that region and hosts the shows only in

English. The important aspect I noticed is that before playing a song she starts talking about it. She continues when the background music plays. She would stop exactly before the first word of the song is played. She would do it again and again without missing the timing. After 3 years when I heard the channel again, she had graduated to host different shows. The RJs now hail from the local place and speak mix of Kannada and English effortlessly.

The second profession is a very interesting one. I stand everyday waiting for my official vehicle at a bus stop. I see an entrepreneur who sells large ice bars. He waits for the truck carrying the ice bars. He would then transport his requirement to the pavement. He would then carry it in a scooter to distribute it to shops. There is a tingle of enthusiasm in his eyes, even if he does the same thing. There is a sense of responsibility when he puts off his cigarette when he reaches for his son. I see a great feeling of achievement when he finishes his work and takes his son in the same scooter for dropping him in the school.

I was having dinner one day in a small restaurant. A young foreigner sat in the table next to me. I was amazed when I heard him speak. He started ordering in Tamil. My friend who was sitting near to him could not resist. He started talking to him. I learned from my friend that the young man was from USA. He is a volunteer in one of the NGOs working for helping HIV patients. He had spent nearly about 5 years in Madurai and learned to speak local dialect fluently. Since he had to work with the residents of the local region, he had to learn the language. He has got accustomed to food and culture. He came back after some time to New Delhi and he searched for this south Indian restaurant. I see him often nowadays and I am very sure he will speak Hindi fluently in future.

All three examples bring out only one single message. The RJ giving information about heritage of Bangalore or the entrepreneur supplying ice bars on time or the young man helping the patients, they all do their work with enthusiasm, application, determination, and commitment. Only social development cannot transform the nation unless there is economic development. Economic development can only fuel social development to uplift the rest of society. Economic development can come only through the great work of you and me. Hence if whatever work we do, if we do the best, we are contributing to the development of the Nation.

We celebrated our 60th Independence Day recently. Only on

this day, we start thinking, what we have done for this country. This is most of the time influenced by movies like "Rang De Basanti" and other nationalistic songs on the television channels. The next day routine catches up with us and we forget all these things. Television channels search for another movie for next year's Independence Day. But if someone asks, what should I do, the answer was found in the oath administered by the President of India to the school children. It roughly says, whatever work you do, do at your best. This is to wipe away the thought that only armed services or social development are the professions that renders direct impact on national development. We are going to see three professions from three different sects of society and understand how they are really important.

It was the time when I was working with a National research laboratory in Bangalore. To spend leisure, I used to listen to the radio. At that time the FM revolution had started. In one particular channel, I liked a Radio Jockey (RJ) for the mere fluency and presence of mind. She would talk for hours and hours in English, which fascinated me. Furthermore, she doesn't belong to that region and hosts the shows only in English. The important aspect I noticed is that before playing a song she starts talking about it. She continues when the background music plays. She would stop exactly before the first word of the song is played. She would do it again and again without missing the timing. After 3 years when I heard the channel again, she had graduated to host different shows. The RJs now hail from the local place and speak mix of Kannada and English effortlessly.

The second profession is a very interesting one. I stand everyday waiting for my official vehicle at a bus stop. I see an entrepreneur who sells large ice bars. He waits for the truck carrying the ice bars. He would then transport his requirement to the pavement. He would then carry it in a scooter to distribute it to shops. There is a tingle of enthusiasm in his eyes, even if he does the same thing. There is a sense of responsibility when he puts off his cigarette when he reaches for his son. I see a great feeling of achievement when he finishes his work and takes his son in the same scooter for dropping him in the school.

I was having dinner one day in a small restaurant. A young foreigner sat in the table next to me. I was amazed when I heard him speak. He started ordering in Tamil. My friend who was sitting near to him could not resist. He started talking to him. I learned from my friend that the young man was from

USA. He is a volunteer in one of the NGOs working for helping HIV patients. He had spent nearly about 5 years in Madurai and learned to speak local dialect fluently. Since he had to work with the residents of the local region, he had to learn the language. He has got accustomed to food and culture. He came back after some time to New Delhi and he searched for this south Indian restaurant. I see him often nowadays and I am very sure he will speak Hindi fluently in future.

All three examples bring out only one single message. The RJ giving information about heritage of Bangalore or the entrepreneur supplying ice bars on time or the young man helping the patients, they all do their work with enthusiasm, application, determination, and commitment. Only social development cannot transform the nation unless there is economic development. Economic development can only fuel social development to uplift the rest of society. Economic development can come only through the great work of you and me. Hence if whatever work we do, if we do the best, we are contributing to the development of the Nation. •

DEPENDENT ARISING

Sunday, April 22, 2007

Paticcasamuppāda (in Pali) or Pratītyasamutpāda (in Sanskrit) is a unique concept to encounter with. An important aspect of Buddhist metaphysics can be translated to Dependent Arising. The concept explains that existence and happenings are interdependent webs of cause and effect. Simply said everything depends on everything else in this Universe. To further explain the concept, we can say that there is a unique purpose of the existence of everything to contribute to the system. So it is believed that everyone should have a certain sense of detachment and transform the energy of desire into awareness and understanding. Let me try to understand the concept by citing two examples in my own life.

My cousin in her very early stage of life was detected with cancer. She went on with the painful treatment for more than a year after detection. I had a chance to meet her during the initial stages of detection and treatment. After that, I had to run with my job to places. Nearly about a year later, I went on to a tour of south Indian cities. The city where my cousin was hospitalized also fell on tour plan. The day I landed in the city was filled with lot of work for me. Finally I managed to find sometime before setting off to next city. I reached the hospital with all eagerness. The time I reached was supposed to be the scheduled visiting time. But I could not see her. Just before I reached there was some complication and she was taken her for emergency care. I waited for more than an hour and left with little disappointment. Later I learned on the same day she came back within ten minutes after I left. The next day I went on with all my work. The day came to halt with dreadful news. The next day I traveled to my hometown, which is about a night's travel from the city where I was. Standing there in the graveyard, I could not comprehend the incidents that brought me there.

The second incident might be closest to a miracle. I have a good friend who drives me sometimes. We share good thoughts on our journey about almost everything. He asks with great concern about my life. However I never have known about his family than he knows about mine. Around two years later I had a chance to perform the holy pilgrimage. For me who have dreamed of pilgrimage towards the later stage of my life, it came as a surprise. As I was making my preparation I had to travel again with my friend. I explained what was keeping me working those days. There was notable silence from him. Then he started saying after so many years of marriage he is yet to blessed with a child. He asked whether I could feed the birds in the holy place during my visit as a mark of special prayer to GOD. I took the money he offered, as I didn't want to challenge his faith. I sincerely fed the birds during my stay. Exactly after a year after I came back from the pilgrimage he was driving for me again. He slowly said that GOD has listened to him and has gifted him with a daughter. With an unexplainable feeling inside, I just asked what is the name?

These two incidents might sound beyond belief. How one might explain the day I when I could not see my cousin but still was nearer to attend the mourning next day. When my pilgrimage itself was a great happening, how it was connected to the birth of a long-awaited child in a family. The reader might think that just because the incidents are put into perspective it seems everything is interconnected. I also don't offer any more rational explanation.

Human intellect has always tried to comprehend the complexity of this universe and essence of life. We often want to believe in concepts to rationalize all the happening of our life. According to me the sheer suspense of the next minute plan is the driving force behind life. If we would like to believe that we exist for a purpose is it not better to use it for improving the lives of people right next to us. The result is a harmonious society where we would be in an advantageous position to live peacefully.

Before closing, I have a great book where I read about the works of Ernest Hemingway. I recently found the latest edition of one of his books and ordered it. I was reading the book and surfing through the television. I ended with one of my favorite serials. One of the characters (who believes in inter-connectedness of life) was saying Ernest Hemingway considered that he could never get out of the shadow of Fyodor Dostoevsky. I had the one author on my hand and went on to buy the book of next one. The scene changes and the character explain the interconnectedness to another man, a priest. The priest looks deeply at him and replies "Please don't mistake coincidence for fate". •

QUORUM SENSING

Wednesday, December 19, 2007

Quorum Sensing is a unique behavior of bacteria. Vibrio Fischeri or V.fischeri is a deep ocean bacterium, which displays intelligent behavior. It produces a protein called lux, which emits light when inside deep-sea fish. Deep-sea fishes' use this bioluminescence to hunt and bacteria live on the hunt. A lot of energy is required to make this protein and use it for glowing. Hence they make this only when inside the deep-sea fish. V.fischeri produces a hormone called Lactone to gauge the critical population density, which is reached when inside the fish. This intelligent behavior is called Quorum Sensing. I had no idea when I read about this from the book (presented by my grandfather) "The Genius Within: Discovering the intelligence of every living thing" by Frank T. Vertosick, JR. that I would come across this topic soon.

I recently visited London to know more about Nanotechnology. The visit took me to the academic centers of Oxford, Cambridge, and Birmingham. I along with my colleagues took time to see around London. It was really interesting to see the smallest police station. It could house only one person and a telephone. One of our colleagues had lived in London, so he introduced background information as we strolled along. Caution: Some of this information could be heard or read before.

We were reaching Cambridge University on one of the days. We started hearing the background of the university formation. In 1209 it was believed a woman was murdered and two of the scholars of the University of Oxford were found nearby. Though the scholars could have received immunity they were hanged as Pope and King were in conflict. Fearing from such an incident the scholars migrated to Cambridge, Reading, and Paris. The location of Cambridge helped to attract scholars from East Anglia, East Midlands, and North; the most prosperous of the regions at that time. King John was reconciled with Pope Innocent III in 1214 and many scholars then returned to Oxford.

We were sitting in the lectures at Cambridge University. A scholar was presenting about the use of Quorum Sensing capability. The intelligent behavior of identifying its own community member reminded me of the incident on the day I landed in London. I had no idea where to take the train to Paddington by Heathrow express, but I was following the signboards. One African traveler had purchased the ticket and was walking down the sub way. While I juggled with my luggage, he offered a smile and said, "It is cold here". Thinking of all the chilling possibilities of talking to a terrorist or fugitive (reading espionage novels in the night has its own effects), I also offered a smile and talked to him. I learned that he was also traveling to London for the first time and had a nice woolen cap to wear for the winter.

The ability to identify to a fellow passenger who is also traveling to London for the first time may not be directly related to Quorum Sensing, but human mind with no mercy maps every single possibility to find pattern. •

MY MOTHER

I see you in the raindrops
Glory in heart
Love filled heart
Letting me remember you
In every small moments
Filling my mind and soul
With all possible love of whole

I see you in the clouds
Showering great wealth
Drizzling high ethics
Letting me follow you
In every difficult moment
Probing my consciousness
With all gracious thoughts

I see you in the lightning
Aggression in speech
Sharp in thoughts
Launching me high
In every march forward
Striking my deeds
With all righteous might

I see you in the nature
Passion in love
Patient in bond
Embracing me with divine shine
In every second I live
Making my life more beautiful
Even heaven can envy about

LEADERSHIP LESSONS

A young man in his casual outfit and with a casual style of walking entered a gathering of highly influential people who were waiting for two old men. One of the old men is a king, who is in a palace and has a beautiful garden adorned by flowers especially and in the fall-winter.

The other old man is an artist who has ripened over the years and then there were those people. The people looked at the young man with a question in their minds, how can he possibly appreciate art and if he can learn anything from here?

But the king had always told him that you can learn anywhere from anyone. He had that confidence, so he quietly settled in a place. Although he knew people around his existence didn't excite anyone as he, in their perspective is not capable of bettering their positions. Even though he himself might think that he has that power and still doesn't want to use that, still people didn't want to pay attention. GOD smiled at them. HE was waiting to touch them with Grace.

The king arrived. Now everyone forgetting the old man rushed to greet the king. But the king knew that the evening belonged to the old man.

As soon as the proceedings started, the anchor started reading out the achievements of the old man. But he was unmoved; he was just trying to adjust his instrument. King was watching; other people were restless; young man motionless … Any lesson?

The concert started. He allowed his fellow men to take the charge. He followed them; allowed them to gather momentum, and remained in shadows. There was a disappointment in other people who have come to hear the old man. King smiled mischievously. There was a flash in the young man's mind.

The great artist traditionally worships one GOD while whom he introduced as his disciple who enjoyed various GOD forms. He proudly presented her as his daughter.

Other people sensed an uneasy contradiction. Old man full of smiles; King winks. Any lesson?

The music started to flow. It was a soul-stirring experience for the young man. He folded his arms and watched the old man in the center. The joy in his face was enormous. He was just visiting his home ground of Almighty and touching everyone with HIS grace. As the rhythm started building, mild music erupted from nowhere and captured the sense of everyone. The same music instrument now played completely different sounds unmatchable and unexplainable. The influential people appeared paralyzed, but still happy, with their sense of ego crushed. The young man, ignorant of music, felt an upward lift. What is this all about?

He was finding it difficult because of his old age and problem with the weather. Whenever his daughter made what perhaps was a mistake, he gently tapped on her shoulder and when she excelled, she showed it by a sign of his hand to others. The young man saw these small actions. The influential people looked for somebody to applaud and immediately followed themselves. Even in that action young man got his message.

The instrument could not fulfill its duty that evening. He looked towards the audience and said, "Today the instrument is not helping me. I feel sorry that I cannot entertain you. But I will try in other ways". With that, he started with a vocal equivalent of the notes, which he might have played in his instrument. The old voice like a lightning struck the people and they were rendered speechless and powerless. Now both the king and the GOD smiled. The young man had two flashes as if from Sun and Moon.

In the end, he announced that next time the artist old man will entertain for sure and urged his team members to complete in time.

A natural leader, a genius, a lover of GOD, displayed one of the wonderfully choreographed acts of leadership mixed with music for all-powerful people gathered there. The crowd now stood, unmoving and clapping.

There was a high tea with neer dosa, masala dosa, poori and so on. The people tried to gather around the King and there were flashes. When some of them can't reach they tried to gather in groups. The rest of them were trying to taste the food. The young man caught hold of an old attendant to talk to. He cannot talk to others, as they were all-powerful. The attendant asked the young man "Kaisa Tha?" (How was it?). The young man told him the five lessons he learned. The attendant smiled and said "Mujhe Maloom Tha!" (I knew).

Now for all curious readers to know about the characters of this short story, •

King   -   President of India Dr. A.P.J. Abdul Kalam

Palace   -   Rashtrapati Bhavan

Garden   -   Mughal Garden

Old man   -   Ustad Bismillah Khan with his Shehnai on
                  4 March 2006, A Jugalbandi Concert

Disciple   -   Dr. Soma Gosh

Leadership Lessons

' in his causal outfit and with a casual style
tered a gathering of highly influential people
ting for two old men. One of the old man is
ves in a palace and has a beautiful garden
owers especially in the fall winter.

d man is an artist who has ripened over
en there were those people. The people
young man with a question in their minds,
possibly appreciate art and if he can learn
here?

had always told him that you can learn
m anyone. He had that confidence, so he

9 789353 914738